Learning the mother tongue

Clare Painter

Series Editor: Frances Christie

Oxford University Press
1989

Oxford University Press
Walton Street, Oxford OX2 6DP

Oxford   New York   Toronto
Delhi   Bombay   Calcutta   Madras   Karachi
Petaling Jaya   Singapore   Hong Kong   Tokyo
Nairobi   Dar es Salaam   Cape Town
Melbourne   Auckland

and associated companies in
Berlin   Ibadan

Oxford English and the *Oxford English* logo are trade marks of
Oxford University Press

ISBN 019 437159 X

© Deakin University 1985, 1989

First published 1985
Second edition 1989

Printed in Hong Kong.

About the author

Clare Painter

Clare Painter was born and brought up in the UK where she took her bachelor's degree in English Literature at the University of Sussex. She married and came to Australia in 1969 after a year spent working in Europe, teaching English to adults and children.

She worked in Sydney for several years, teaching English to adult migrants, and began to study linguistics at the University of Sydney. These studies were motivated partly by a wish to appreciate the theoretical sources of second language teaching methodology, and partly by a much more general interest in the nature of language.

She recently completed a monograph entitled *Into the Mother Tongue* (F. Pinter, London, 1984); this is based on her MA thesis in linguistics, undertaken at the University of Sydney, and explores the first stages of language development, based on a case study of her eldest son's early development. She has been involved in the teaching of linguistics for several years and is currently working as a tutor in the Department of Linguistics at Sydney University. As well as being concerned with the development of linguistic theory, she is interested in both mother tongue and English as a Second Language applications of linguistics in education.

Foreword

In a sense, educational interest in language is not new. Studies of rhetoric and of grammar go back as far as the Greeks; in the English-speaking countries, studies of the classical languages, and more recently of English itself, have had a well established place in educational practice. Moreover, a number of the issues which have aroused the most passionate debates about how to develop language abilities have tended to remain, resurfacing at various points in history in somewhat different formulations perhaps, but nonetheless still there, and still lively.

Of these issues, probably the most lively has been that concerning the extent to which explicit knowledge about language on the part of the learner is a desirable or a useful thing. But the manner in which discussion about this issue has been conducted has often been allowed to obscure other and bigger questions: questions, for example, both about the nature of language as an aspect of human experience, and about language as a resource of fundamental importance in the building of human experience. The tendency in much of the western intellectual tradition has been to dissociate language and experience, in such a way that language is seen as rather neutral, merely serving to 'carry' the fruits of experience. Whereas in this view language is seen as a kind of 'conduit', subservient to experience in various ways, an alternative view, as propounded in the books in this series, would argue that language is itself not only a part of experience, but intimately involved in the manner in which we construct and organise experience. As such, it is never neutral, but deeply implicated in building meaning. One's notions concerning how to teach about language will differ quite markedly, depending upon the view one adopts concerning language and experience. In fact, though discussions concerning teaching about language can sometimes be interesting, in practice many such discussions have proved theoretically ill-founded and barren, serving merely to perpetuate a number of unhelpful myths about language.

The most serious and confusing of these myths are those which would suggest we can dissociate language from meaning — form from function, or form from 'content'. Where such myths apply, teaching about language becomes a matter of teaching about 'language rules' — normally grammatical rules — and as history has demonstrated over the years, such teaching rapidly degenerates into the arid pursuit of parts of speech and the parsing of isolated sentences. Meaning, and the critical role of language in the building of meaning, are simply overlooked, and the kinds of knowledge about language made available to the learner are of a very limited kind.

The volumes in this series of monographs devoted to language education in my view provide a much better basis upon which to address questions related to the teaching about language than has been the case anywhere in the English-speaking world for some time now. I make this claim for several reasons, one of the most important being that the series never sought directly to establish a model for teaching about language at all. On the contrary, it sought to establish a principled model of language, which, once properly articulated, allows us to address many questions of an educational nature, including those to do with teaching about language. To use Halliday's term (1978), such a model sees language primarily as a 'social semiotic', and as a resource for meaning, centrally involved in the processes by which human beings negotiate, construct and change the nature of social experience. While the series certainly does not claim to have had the last word on these and related subjects, I believe it does do much to set a new educational agenda — one which enables us to look closely at the role of language both in living and in learning: one which, moreover, provides a basis upon which to decide those kinds of teaching and learning about language which may make a legitimate contribution to the development of the learner.

I have said that arguments to do with teaching about language have been around for a long time: certainly as long as the two hundred years of white settlement in Australia. In fact, coincidentally, just as the first settlers were taking up their enforced residence in the Australian colony of New South Wales, Lindley Murray was preparing his *English Grammar* (1795), which, though not the only volume produced on the subject in the eighteenth century, was certainly the best. Hundreds of school grammars that were to appear in Britain and Australia for the next century at least, were to draw very heavily upon what Murray had written. The parts of speech, parsing and sentence analysis, the latter as propounded by Morell (an influential inspector of schools in England), were the principal elements in the teaching about language in the Australian colonies, much as they were in England throughout the century. By the 1860s and 1870s the Professor of Classics and Logic at Sydney University, Charles Badham, who had arrived from England in 1867, publicly disagreed with the examining authorities in New South Wales concerning the teaching of grammar. To the contemporary reader there is a surprising modernity about many of his objections, most notably his strongly held conviction that successful control of one's language is learned less as a matter of committing to memory the parts of speech and the principles of parsing, than as a matter of frequent opportunity for use.

Historically, the study by which issues of use had been most effectively addressed had been that of rhetoric, in itself quite old in the English-speaking tradition, dating back at least to the sixteenth century. Rhetorical studies flourished in the eighteenth century, the best known works on the subject being George Campbell's *The Philosophy of Rhetoric* (1776), and Hugh Blair's *Lectures on Rhetoric and Belles Lettres* (1783), while in the nineteenth century Richard Whately published his work, *Elements of Rhetoric* (1828). As the nineteenth century proceeded, scholarly work on rhetoric declined, as was testified by the markedly inferior but nonetheless influential works of Alexander Bain (*English Composition and Rhetoric*, 1866; Revised version, 1887). Bain, in fact, did much to corrupt and destroy the older rhetorical traditions, primarily because he lost sight of the need for a basic concern with meaning in language. Bain's was the century of romanticism after all: on the one hand, Matthew Arnold was extolling the civilising influence of English literature in the development of children; on the other hand, there was a tendency towards suspicion, even contempt, for those who wanted to take a scholarly look at the linguistic organisation of texts, and at the ways in which they were structured for the building of meaning. In 1921, Ballard (who was an expert witness before the Newbolt Enquiry on the teaching of English), wrote a book called *Teaching the Mother Tongue*, in which he noted among other things, that unfortunately in England at least rhetorical studies had become associated with what were thought to be rather shallow devices for persuasion and argument. The disinclination to take seriously the study of the rhetorical organisation of texts gave rise to a surprisingly unhelpful tradition for the teaching of literature, which is with us yet in many places: 'civilising' it might be, but it was *not* to be the object of systematic study, for such study would in some ill-defined way threaten or devalue the work of literature itself.

A grammarian like Murray had never been in doubt about the relationship of grammar and rhetoric. As he examined it, grammar was concerned with the syntax of the written English sentence: it was not concerned with the study of 'style', about which he wrote a short appendix in his original grammar, where his debt to the major rhetoricians of the period was apparent. Rhetorical studies, especially as discussed by Campbell for instance, did address questions of 'style', always from the standpoint of a recognition of the close relationship of language to the socially created purpose in using language. In fact, the general model of language as discussed by Campbell bore some relationship to the model taken up in this series, most notably in its commitment to register.

The notion of register proposes a very intimate relationship of text to context: indeed, so intimate is that relationship, it is asserted, that the one can only be interpreted by reference to the other. Meaning is realised in language (in the form of text), which is thus shaped or patterned in response to the context of situation in which it is used. To study language then, is to concentrate upon exploring how it is systematically patterned towards important social ends. The linguistic theory adopted here is that of systemic linguistics. Such a linguistic theory is itself also a social theory, for it proposes firstly, that it is in the nature of human behaviour to build reality and/or experience through complex semiotic processes, and secondly, that the principal semiotic system available to humans is their language. In this sense, to study language is to explore some of the most important and pervasive of the processes by which human beings build their world.

I originally developed the volumes in this series as the basis of two major off campus courses in Language Education taught in the Master's degree program at Deakin University, Victoria, Australia. To the best of my knowledge, such courses, which are designed primarily for teachers and teacher educators, are the first of their kind in the world, and while they actually appeared in the mid 1980s, they emerge from work in language education which has been going on in Australia for some time. This included the national Language Development Project, to which Michael Halliday was consultant, and whose work I co-ordinated throughout its second, productive phase. (This major project was initiated by the Commonwealth Government's Curriculum Development Centre, Canberra, in the 1970s, and involved the co-operation of curriculum development teams from all Australian states in developing language curriculum materials. Its work was not completed because of political changes which caused the activities of the Curriculum Development Centre to be wound down.) In the 1980s a number of conferences have been held fairly regularly in different parts of Australia, all of them variously exploring aspects of language education, and leading to the publication of a number of conference reports. They include: Frances Christie (ed.), *Language and the Social Construction of Experience* (Deakin University, 1983); Brendan Bartlett and John Carr (eds.), *Language in Education Workshop: a Report of Proceedings* (Centre for Research and Learning, Brisbane C.A.E., Mount Gravatt Campus, Brisbane, 1984); Ruqaiya Hasan (ed.), *Discourse on Discourse* (Applied Linguistics Association of Australia, Occasional Papers, Number 7, 1985); Clare Painter and J.R. Martin (eds.), *Writing to Mean: Teaching Genres across the Curriculum* (Applied Linguistics Association of Australia, Occasional Papers, Number 9, 1986); Linda Gerot, Jane Oldenburg and Theo Van Leeuwen (eds.), *Language and Socialisation: Home and School* (in preparation). All these activities have contributed to the building of a climate of opinion and a tradition of thinking about language which made possible the development of the volumes in this series.

While it is true that the developing tradition of language education which these volumes represent does, as I have noted, take up some of the concerns of the older rhetorical studies, it nonetheless also looks forward, pointing to ways of examining language which were not available in earlier times. For example, the notion of language as a social semiotic, and its associated conception of experience or reality as socially built and constantly subject to processes of transformation, finds very much better expression today than would have been possible before, though obviously much more requires to be said about this than can be dealt with in these volumes. In addition, a functionally driven view of language is now available, currently most completely articulated in Halliday's *An Introduction to Functional Grammar* (1985), which offers ways of understanding the English language in a manner that Murray's Grammar could not have done.

Murray's Grammar confined itself to considerations of the syntax of the written English sentence. It did not have anything of use to say about spoken language, as opposed to written language, and, equally, it provided no basis upon which to explore a unit other than the sentence, whether that be the paragraph, or, even more importantly, the total text. The preoccupation with the written sentence reflected the pre-eminent position being accorded to the written word by Murray's time, leading to disastrous consequences since, that is the diminished value accorded to spoken language, especially in educational practices. In Murray's work, the lack of a direct relationship between the study of grammar on the one hand, and that of 'style', on the other hand, was, as I have already noted, to be attributed to his view that it was the rhetorician who addressed wider questions relating to the text. In the tradition in which he worked, in fact, grammar looked at syntactic rules divorced from considerations of meaning or social purpose.

By contrast, Halliday's approach to grammar has a number of real strengths, the first of which is the fact that its basis is semantic, not syntactic: that is to say, it is a semantically driven grammar, which, while not denying that certain principles of syntax do apply, seeks to consider and identify the role of various linguistic items in any text in terms of their function in building meaning. It is for this reason that its practices for interpreting and labelling various linguistic items and groupings are functionally based, not syntactically based. There is in other words, no dissociation of 'grammar' on the one hand and 'semantics' or meaning on the other. A second strength of Halliday's approach is that it is not uniquely interested in written language, being instead committed to the study of both the spoken and written modes, and to an explanation of the differences between the two, in such a way that each is illuminated because of its contrast with the other. A third and final strength of the systemic functional grammar is that it permits useful movement across the text, addressing the manner in which linguistic patternings are built up for the construction of the overall text in its particular 'genre', shaped as it is in response to the context of situation which gave rise to it.

Halliday's functional grammar lies behind all ten volumes in this series, though one other volume, by Michael Christie, called *Aboriginal perspectives on experience and learning: the role of language in Aboriginal Education*, draws upon somewhat different if still compatible perspectives in educational and language theory to develop its arguments. The latter volume, is available directly from Deakin University. In varying ways, the volumes in this series provide a helpful introduction to much that is more fully dealt with in Halliday's Grammar, and I commend the series to the reader who wants to develop some sense of the ways such a body of linguistic theory can be applied to educational questions. A version of the grammar specifically designed for teacher education remains to be written, and while I cherish ambitions to begin work on such a version soon, I am aware that others have similar ambitions − in itself a most desirable development.

While I have just suggested that the reader who picks up any of the volumes in this series should find ways to apply systemic linguistic theory to educational theory, I want to argue, however, that what is offered here is more than merely a course in applied linguistics, legitimate though such a course might be. Rather, I want to claim that this is a course in educational linguistics, a term of importance because it places linguistic study firmly at the heart of educational enquiry. While it is true that a great deal of linguistic research of the past, where it did not interpret language in terms of interactive, social processes, or where it was not grounded in a concern for meaning, has had little of relevance to offer education, socially relevant traditions of linguistics like that from which systemics is derived, do have a lot to contribute. How that contribution should be articulated is quite properly a matter of development in partnership between educationists, teachers and linguistics, and a great deal has yet to be done to achieve such articulation.

I believe that work in Australia currently is making a major contribution to the development of a vigorous educational linguistics, not all of it of course in a systemic framework. I would note here the important work of such people as J.R. Martin, Joan Rothery, Suzanne Eggins and Peter Wignell of the University of Sydney, investigating children's writing development; the innovatory work of Brian Gray and his colleagues a few years ago in developing language programs for Aboriginal children in central Australia, and more recently his work with other groups in Canberra; the recent work of Beth Graham, Michael Christie and Stephen Harris, all of the Northern Territory Department of Education, in developing language programs for Aboriginal children; the important work of John Carr and his colleagues of the Queensland Department of Education in developing new perspectives upon language in the various language curriculum guidelines they have prepared for their state; the contributions of Jenny Hammond of the University of Wollongong, New South Wales, in her research into language development in schools, as well as the various programs in which she teaches; research being undertaken by Ruqaiya Hasan and Carmel Cloran of Macquarie University, Sydney, into children's language learning styles in the transition years from home to school; investigations by Linda Gerot, also of Macquarie University, into classroom discourse in the secondary school, across a number of different subjects; and the work of Pam Gilbert of James Cook University, Townsville, in Queensland, whose interests are both in writing in the secondary school, and in language and gender.

The signs are that a coherent educational linguistics is beginning to appear around the world, and I note with pleasure the appearance of two new and valuable international journals: *Language and Education*, edited by David Corson of Massey University, New Zealand, and *Linguistics in Education*, edited by David Bloome, of the University of Massachusetts. Both are committed to the development of an educational linguistics, to which many traditions of study, linguistic, semiotic and sociological, will no doubt make an important contribution. Such an educational linguistics is long overdue, and in what are politically difficult times, I suggest such a study can make a major contribution to the pursuit of educational equality of opportunity, and to attacking the wider social problems of equity and justice. Language is a political institution: those who are wise in its ways, capable of using it to shape and serve important personal and social goals, will be the ones who are 'empowered' (to use a fashionable word): able, that is, not merely to participate effectively *in* the world, but able also *to act upon it*, in the sense that they can strive for significant social change. Looked at in these terms, provision of appropriate language education programs is a profoundly important matter, both in ensuring equality of educational opportunity, and in helping to develop those who are able and willing to take an effective role in democratic processes of all kinds.

One of the most encouraging measures of the potential value of the perspectives open to teachers taking up an educational linguistics of the kind offered in these monographs, has been the variety of teachers attracted to the courses of which they form a part, and the ways in which these teachers have used what they have learned in undertaking research papers for the award of the master's degree. They include, for example, secondary teachers of physics, social science, geography and English, specialists in teaching English as a second language to migrants and specialists in teaching English to Aboriginal people, primary school teachers, a nurse educator, teachers of illiterate adults, and language curriculum consultants, as well as a number of teacher educators with specialist responsibilities in teaching language education. For many of these people the perspectives offered by an educational linguistics are both new and challenging, causing them to review and change aspects of their teaching practices in various ways. Coming to terms with a semantically driven grammar is in itself quite demanding, while there is often considerable effort involved to bring to conscious awareness the ways in which we use language for the realisation of different meanings. But the effort is plainly worth it, principally because of the added sense of control and direction it can give teachers interested to work at fostering and developing students who are independent and confident in using language for the achievement of various goals. Those people for whom these books have proved helpful, tend to say that they have achieved a stronger and richer appreciation of language and how it works than they had before; that because they know considerably more about language themselves, they are able to intervene much more effectively in directing and guiding those whom they teach; that because they have a better sense of the relationship of language and 'content' than they had before, they can better guide their students into control of the 'content' of the various subjects for which they are responsible; and finally, that because they have an improved sense of how to direct language learning, they are able to institute new assessment policies, negotiating, defining and clarifying realistic goals for their students. By any standards, these are considerable achievements.

As I draw this Foreword to a close, I should perhaps note for the reader's benefit the manner in which students doing course work with me are asked to read the monographs in this series, though I should stress that the books were deliberately designed to be picked up and read in any order one likes. In the first of the two semester courses, called *Language and Learning*, students are asked to read the following volumes in the order given:

Frances Christie — *Language education*
Clare Painter — *Learning the mother tongue*
M.A.K. Halliday & Ruqaiya Hasan — *Language, context, and text: aspects of language in a social-semiotic perspective*
J.L. Lemke — *Using language in the classroom*
then either,
M.A.K. Halliday — *Spoken and written language*
or,
Ruqaiya Hasan — *Linguistics, language, and verbal art.*

The following four volumes, together with the one by Michael Christie, mentioned above, belong to the second course called *Sociocultural Aspects of Language and Education*, and they may be read by the students in any order they like, though only three of the five need be selected for close study:

David Butt — *Talking and thinking: the patterns of behaviour*
Gunther Kress — *Linguistic processes in sociocultural practice*
J.R. Martin — *Factual writing: exploring and challenging social reality*
Cate Poynton — *Language and gender: making the difference*

References

Bain, A., *An English Grammar* (Longman, Roberts and Green, London, 1863).

Bain, A., *English Composition and Rhetoric*, revised in two Parts — *Part 1, Intellectual Elements of Style*, and *Part 11, Emotional Qualities of Style* (Longman, Green and Company, London, 1887).

Ballard, P., *Teaching the Mother Tongue* (Hodder & Stoughton, London, 1921).

Blair, H., *Lectures on Rhetoric and Belles Lettres, Vols. 1 and 11* (W. Strahan and T. Cadell, London, 1783).

Campbell, G., (new ed.), *The Philosophy of Rhetoric* (T. Tegg and Son, London, 1838). Originally published (1776).

Halliday, M.A.K., *Language as social semiotic: the social interpretation of language and meaning* (Edward Arnold, London, 1978).

Halliday, M.A.K., *An Introduction to Functional Grammar* (Edward Arnold, London, 1985).

Murray, Lindley, *English Grammar* (1795), Facsimile Reprint No. 106 (Menston, Scolar Press, 1968).

Contents

Introduction

It is a commonplace, both of our everyday commonsense ideas about language, and of educational and linguistic theory, that before the age of five any normal child has mastered his or her native language (with the exception of literacy skills of course). This being the case, the language is seen as available to him or her as a tool for learning other things once he or she gets to school. In this book, we will be exploring the way the child comes to this linguistic achievement in the first few years of life.

The most important reason for doing this is to come to an understanding of the essential nature of language itself. If we observe the growth of language abilities from their very beginning, then we have the best chance of understanding how (and why) the fully fledged adult language works as it does. And without a clear understanding of this, we will be in no position to judge the merits or demerits of various educational proposals, either for the development of children's language itself, or for using language more generally in an institutional setting.

Insights gained from an examination of pre-school language development will, I hope, put us in a better position to assess in what sense and to what degree it is true to say that a two-, three-, or five-year-old has 'acquired' the mother tongue. And we will be in a better position to judge whether it makes sense to separate language and 'content' as is so commonly done in educational contexts.

If we wish to trace the development in a child's life from being a prelinguistic baby to a competent language user, then the obvious place to start our investigation is when the infant first begins to use language, in however limited a way. It may therefore come as a surprise to find that it is not an entirely straightforward matter to determine at what point one should begin an account of language development, nor what kind of measure should be used to assess linguistic progress.

Typical parents, of course, have no such problems, and will state authoritatively that their child began to talk at some precise moment—usually on the basis that this was when the first word was uttered by the child. However, linguists, who make the study of language their business, have chosen both later and earlier points as heralding the beginning of productive language. In doing this they have been directed by their different theoretical preconceptions, and in the following section I shall refer to the most prominent trends in child language research in recent times. In this way, the research and attitudes I shall be putting forward in the rest of the coursebook will be placed into some kind of intellectual context for you.

Chapter 1

Child language studies: a brief overview

Language as a syntactic system

During the 1960s, under the influence of Noam Chomsky and his theory of TRANSFORMATIONAL GRAMMAR (Chomsky, 1957, 1965), language was technically defined as a set of rules describing different sentence structures. The essence of language was taken to be its syntactic structure, and so the most interesting starting point for language proper was the production of the first two-word structures—the beginning of syntax. Thus, the children most intensively studied at this time were in their second or third year of life (see Braine, 1963; Brown & Bellugi, 1964)

In transformational theory, as articulated at the time, there were two sets of rules that described language: phrase structure rules, which describe a limited number of abstract linguistic patterns, known as deep structures; and transformational rules, which converted these abstract deep structures into the variety of surface structures of actual speech. Developing language was therefore seen as a matter of acquiring these two sets of rules. But the linguistic data to which a child is exposed consist solely of surface structures (i.e. language as uttered), and surface structures do not directly reveal either deep structures or transformational rules. It was therefore a logical concomitant of the theory to propose that in some sense 'knowledge' of the rules of linguistic structure is innate in the child—the 'innateness hypothesis'.

In this theory, the system of language is therefore seen as too complex for it to be learnable from exposure to the phenomenon. Language development is seen as taking place smoothly as a result of intellectual growth, rather than because of the nature of language itself, or any role it might play in that cognitive growth. With the increasing complexity of 'cognitive structures', increasingly complex linguistic structures are to be expected. Some researchers have even endeavoured to find direct parallels between particular cognitive skills and mastery of particular linguistic structures. For example, one experiment sought to demonstrate a relationship between the capacity to manipulate and stack cups of varying sizes on the one hand, and the linguistic capacity to use dependent relative clauses on the other (Greenfield et al., 1972).

Not only the innateness hypothesis, but this whole approach to language focuses on the individual and his or her mental apparatus. One effect of this orientation was a lack of interest in environmental factors such as the kind of interactions in which a child engages when producing language, or the kind of language to which a young child is exposed. Correspondingly, linguistic progress was measured by mean length of utterance (MLU) produced by the child, rather than in other terms, such as the appropriateness of his or her contributions to conversational discourse.

The mean length of utterance is a formal measure of linguistic progress.

Language as a semantic system

Chomsky considered the system of syntactic rules that constituted a language to be something self-contained and accessible to investigation. He followed the tradition of the influential American linguist, Leonard Bloomfield, and his structuralist school, in regarding the area of meaning in language as far less amenable to rigorous scientific analysis than syntactic or phonological structures.

Meaning in language was held to be inaccessible to rigorous investigation.

However, many linguists became dissatisfied with this restrictive approach to their discipline, and psychologists and others studying child language were not always content to accept that no explanation for the swift mastery of language need be sought beyond the individual's supposed inborn knowledge of linguistic rules.

One way of approaching meaning in language adopted by some (Ingram, 1971; Schlesinger, 1971; Greenfield & Smith, 1976) was to regard deep structures as being semantic rather than syntactic in nature. In the context of child language research, this meant interpreting an utterance like *Daddy come* as a basic Agent + Action structure, rather than a subject + verb one. The assumption was that 'semantic structure' exists transparently in the real world, and that the child's task is one of matching words to this observable reality: 'Children might use the context of real world events as a structured framework which could be gradually filled in with verbal forms' (Greenfield & Smith, 1976, p.30).

One or two assumptions underlying this approach need pointing out here. One is the assumption that there is a simple isomorphism (a one-to-one correspondence), between any 'bit' of extralinguistic reality and a linguistic form. This implies, for example, that there is no difference between languages in the way that they read or encode the 'same' reality. It also implies that there is no difference between the interpretation of a real world event made by a very young child, and that made by adult speakers of the language. Such an approach inevitably tends to analyse children's utterances as failed, unsatisfactory, or incomplete attempts at adult speech. Finally, I would suggest that to regard matching words to reality in this way as the sum of the child's task is an over-simplified view both of what language is and of what we do with it.

Although those who viewed language as semantic structure saw themselves as departing quite radically from the Chomskyan tradition, there are in fact many similarities in their approaches to language and language development. In both cases, language is regarded as a self-contained set of rules defining structures (rather than, for example, a kind of communicative behaviour), and in both cases children's utterances tend to be viewed as a version of adult speech rather than as a system of the child's, functioning to serve his or her own peculiar needs.

One of the gains of the semantic approach to child language was that greater attention was paid to the situational context in which speech occurred. (This was necessary in order to determine whether a named object was to be regarded as an Agent or Patient or Location element in any particular utterance.) It was not, however, until the 1970s that the **linguistic** environment for early utterances became the focus of attention. Chomsky had stated that the language the child hears during his or her language-learning years is a degenerate sample, full of false starts, hesitations, self-interruptions, and the like. This opinion had been accepted uncritically by many linguists, although it was not based on any empirical examination of speech addressed to babies and children.

The Agent is the 'doer'; the Patient has something 'done' to him/her/it; the Location element refers to the place where something happens.

Language as interaction

'Motherese'

In the 1970s, there was a burst of interest in, and research into, the language spoken to young children—a style of speech that became known as baby-talk, or 'motherese' (see Newport, 1976; Snow & Ferguson, 1977). This work posed questions such as the following: Are there special ways in which mothers talk to very young infants? If so, what are they? And how might they be relevant to the child's learning of language?

Other paradigms had seen the language learner solely as an individual who gradually achieves cognitive, and hence linguistic, maturity in the process of coming to grips with the nature of the real world. By contrast, this kind of research took it as of paramount importance that language learning is something that the child achieves in the course of interacting with other people. It stressed the importance of the linguistic, rather than the material, environment, and saw this as the factor enabling the child to learn language swiftly and successfully.

Although many of those working in this area did not have any very sophisticated means of analysing discourse, they were able to arrive at some relatively firm conclusions. They found that the language addressed to infants is by no means full of hesitations, false starts, and obscurity. On the contrary, mothers use clear, well-structured utterances, and work very hard at verbal communication with their children. This involves them in frequent rephrasings and repetitions, clear articulation, arresting intonation patterns, and making the most, conversationally, of any contribution by the child.

A further finding was that mothers 'fine-tune' their speech to match the changing level of competence of their children, producing more complex structural forms and fewer repetitions as the child's command of the language increases (Cross, 1977; Snow & Ferguson, 1977). Such findings strongly suggest that the fact that speech occurs in interactive settings is highly relevant to the fact that it is learned, and learned in a comparatively short period of time.

Speech act theory

The late 1960s and the 1970s also saw some new theoretical approaches to language, which focused on its interactive aspects, rather than defining it in terms of form, as a set of structures.

The work of the philosopher, John Austin, and his SPEECH ACT THEORY was most influential here. Austin (1962) had pointed out that utterances might be classified as various kinds of speech act according to their communicative function. That is to say, the sentence *My car is a Holden* can be seen as having a descriptive function, conveying a fact, whereas *Open the door* or *I need a bigger nail* are both speech acts having a directive function, aimed at getting the addressee to do something—and so on.

In order to determine the function of an utterance, it is obviously necessary to pay considerable attention to the speaker's non-verbal behaviour, and to the general speech situation, since these factors may indicate a speaker's intentions more clearly than the actual syntactic form of what is said. Moreover, if language is defined in terms of communicative behaviour rather than syntactic form, then it is possible to link it with other kinds of behaviour, including pre-linguistic behaviour. One of the primary effects, then, of this change of focus, as it concerns child language studies, has been to allow much younger infants to be studied (see Bruner, 1975; Dore, 1975; Bates, 1979; Waterson & Snow, 1978).

Infant psychology

In addition, a number of psychologists have recently become interested in neonatal and infant behaviour, and have adopted a new approach in this field. Their methods consist of observations of the vocal and other behaviour of infants in as natural a situation as possible. This work focuses on spontaneous behaviours rather than data elicited from contrived, experimental situations, and has greatly contributed to our understanding of the prelinguistic child. (See Lock, 1978 for a valuable collection of papers here.)

The kinds of earlier behaviour that can be linked with language development include the gazing and attention-exchanging behaviour of infants, the establishment of turn-taking rituals, and the way the latter lead to games with the adult where different roles are established and perhaps marked verbally in due course.

Functional theories of language, such as speech act theory or pragmatics—the study of rules of language use—often look at development as an increase in the child's repertoire of speech acts—evidence of being able to do more things with language. Typical early speech acts recognised are such things as labelling, protest, refusal, repetition, request, etc. Development can also be seen in terms of learning to convey, by conventional linguistic forms, meanings previously conveyed by gesture and non-language vocalisations (see Bruner, 1975), or by verbal, but non-grammatical, expressions (see Dore, 1975).

meaning-oriented
assessments of
linguistic progress

6

Chapter 2

Systemic theory: language and metafunction

In Chapters 3 and 4 of this book, I shall be discussing the language development of my own son, Hal, in the first two years of his life. This will be with a view to exploring with you what was involved in his becoming a speaker of his mother tongue, and what we can learn from that about the phenomenon of language and what it means for anyone to be a language user. It should, however, be apparent from Chapter 1 that no such investigation can take place without some preconception as to what language is, and in this section I propose to sketch out some of the ideas about language that have informed my own research in this field.

If we consider language simply in terms of an abstract, highly complex system of interrelated rules of sound and syntactic patterns, then the ability of every normal child to gain control of the system within a few years of birth is little short of a mystery. And an attempt to explain the mystery has to be directed at exploring the child's cognitive apparatus. This was the inclination of transformational theorists, and the child language data they explored were often elicited in experimental situations in order to collect and focus on specific linguistic or cognitive structures.

However, if, as I would suggest, we accept that language is a social phenomenon, we are led to observe that the interactions engaged in by the infant are distinctive, and relevant to language learning. This leads us to suppose that the way communication takes place between the child and his or her intimates—parents, care-givers, siblings—at least partly accounts for how language comes to be learned. Such a claim would be accepted by all the various 'interactionalist' approaches, including that of systemic theory, which is the linguistic theory I shall be adopting to explicate language development in the rest of this book.

SYSTEMIC THEORY, as developed most prominently by M.A.K. Halliday (1976, 1978, 1984), is distinctive in being a functional theory in a more profound sense than is speech act theory. Like the latter, it is functional in that we are interested in what someone does when making an utterance—in whether the utterance is used to control the addressee, to provide information, to make a promise, etc. But, unlike other theorists, Halliday has suggested that the requirements that humans have placed on language have given it a certain organisational

Language is a social phenomenon learned in interaction.

Extensive references to Halliday's work and its evolution appear in the other books in this series.

7

shape, reflecting just a few basic functions of language, which he calls METAFUNCTIONS. The fact that language is organised in terms of these metafunctions makes it readily learnable by the infant, while conversely, it is by looking at how language evolves in the history of the individual that its functional organisation can be most clearly demonstrated. This is why it is of great interest to explore the early years of language development, even if our applied interests focus on language in later life.

I have said that language is organised in the way that it is because of what we need to do with it. One thing we obviously do with language is to talk about things, to make reference to the world of experience (including 'inner', mental experience). This is the function focused on by 'semantic' theories of language—our ability to make reference to objects, events, relations of time, place, cause, etc. In systemic theory this is characterised as the experiential function of language, or the EXPERIENTIAL METAFUNCTION.

the experiential metafunction of language

Equally uncontroversial now is the recognition that, on the whole, language is used to communicate with someone else. As human beings, we talk to each other and expect those we address to take different utterances in various ways: as instructions, contradictions, questions, statements, commands, etc.—different moves and sub-moves in exchanges either of information or of goods and services. This is the function of language that focuses on the status of an utterance as an interaction with another person, and so it is termed the INTERPERSONAL METAFUNCTION. This is the function of language that speech act theory pays greatest attention to.

the interpersonal metafunction

There is a third function of language recognised within systemic theory, which is one intrinsic to language—that of being coherent as text. A text—whether it be a casual conversation or a work of art—is never a random set of sentences, but something whose component parts are relevant to the context, both linguistic and situational. This intrinsic function is termed the TEXTUAL METAFUNCTION.

the textual metafunction

What does it mean to say that language is organised in terms of these three functions? It means that the grammar of a language has three components, each of which is a set of meaning choices. There are a number of experiential meaning choices such as that between an action meaning (*run*, *break*) and a cognition meaning (*see*, *think*). There are interpersonal meaning choices, such as the choice of questioning as against answering, or the choice of using an expression of attitude like *unfortunately* in *Unfortunately, it rained*. In addition, there are textual options, such as the choice of which element should begin the sentence, or which should receive intonational stress, with regard to the previous sentence or utterance.

Each of these sets of meaning options constitutes a relatively distinct part of the grammar, but choices are made from each set whenever we speak. (These choices are not to be seen as conscious, psychological choices, of course.)

To make all this clearer, let us take the utterance *Did Jim take the book?* This clause makes reference to an action, a person (who performed the action), and an object (which suffered the action). All this concerns the experiential nature of the clause, which would be exactly the same for *Jim took the book*. The elements of either clause

8

can be analysed into the same three parts: Actor (*Jim*), Process (*take*), Goal (*book*).

The difference between the two is one of demanding information in the first case, as against giving it in the second—in other words in its interpersonal status. It is the position of the Subject element that tells us which interpersonal structure is involved: in the interrogative questioning form, the Subject follows the first part of the verb, while in the declarative, it precedes it.

An element such as *the* is obviously involved in linking the utterance to some context, and the difference between two forms identical in both experiential and interpersonal aspects, such as *Was the book taken by Jim?* and *Did Jim take the book?* can also be related to the textual function of creating links with the larger discourse, rendering the utterance a relevant one.

The different meaning components of the grammar are thus each producing a distinct structural patterning, and all three co-exist in any single utterance produced. In this sense, then, the language is organised into metafunctional components.

It was with this conception of language as organised in terms of these three fundamental functions that I approached the study of language development that I shall refer to here. Moreover, Halliday's own account of language development (Halliday, 1975) is also the chief source for many of the ideas I shall be putting to you here.

Chapter 3
Phase I of language development

Although I have tried to sketch out some of the main theoretical claims about language made by systemic theory, it is by observing the development of this tri-partite metafunctional system in the early life of the individual that the nature of language is perhaps most clearly revealed.

In this and the next three chapters, I shall therefore give some account of how my son, Hal, learned his mother tongue in the first two years of life (see Painter, 1984 for a more detailed account). However, to make the description more succinct and less complicated, I shall focus only on the development of the experiential and interpersonal metafunctions, ignoring for the most part, that of the textual metafunction.

Since the theory suggests that we are interested in the evolution of these general metafunctional meaning areas, it makes sense to see the beginning of the story as arising at the point when vocal sounds made by the child are first used in a meaningful way. A communication system of sorts can be recognised once there is a 'constant relation between the content and the expression' (Halliday, 1975, p.14). In other words, for a sound to have some symbolic import, it must always carry the same identifiable meaning.

This may well sound like an account of 'first words' and how to distinguish imperfect imitations of words from random coos and cries. But this is not the point at all, for a number of studies (for example, Halliday, 1975; Bates, 1979; Carter, 1979) have now demonstrated that the child in his or her first year of life creates his or her own small set of meaning—sound symbols without reference to the mother tongue. This early symbol system is termed by Halliday (1975) the PROTO-LANGUAGE.

Hal's protolanguage

What kind of meanings could an infant in the first year of life be expressing? Let us look at the symbols (or signs, as Halliday calls them) used by Hal when he was a little over nine months old, about two months after he first began to create such signs.

Signs used by Hal at nine and a half months

[ ] enclose phonetic symbols when they appear in isolation in the text; the symbols are those of the International Phonetic Alphabet (alphabet of the International Phonetic Association).

1. [ga]—'gah'
This was spoken in two ways and used in two kinds of situation.
(a) One kind of situation was when he was manipulating some object or toy. On these occasions he spoke without emphasis and without looking up from his task, as if to say just 'I'm busy with this'.
(b) In the other kind of situation, he was also handling an object but would hold it aloft and make eye contact with his addressee before saying [ga] loudly and forcefully, as if to say 'see what I'm doing' or 'see what I've got'.
2. [x:]—a soft hissing at the back of the mouth
This was uttered with a smile when a familiar person came into view for the first time, as if to say 'that's nice—it's you'.
3. [gaɪ gaɪ gaɪ]—'guy-guy-guy'
This was sung softly to himself as he lay back after finishing a bottle of milk, as if to say 'now I feel content'.
4. [amamama]—'umm-umm-ummu'
This sound was used while Hal made reaching gestures towards food or other desired objects. Usually his gaze oscillated between an addressee and the desired object, and he persisted with the sign until he was given the object or realised tearfully that he was not going to get it.

When we consider this little set of symbols, we can see that 1(a), [ga], and 3, [gaɪ gaɪ gaɪ], occurred in what we might call non-social situations, and were concerned respectively with expressing interest in the environment and contented reaction to some aspect of it. Halliday has suggested the term PERSONAL FUNCTION for signs of this kind, and because these two can both be interpreted in terms of one function, they can be represented as more closely related to each other than to any other symbol. This can be indicated schematically by linking them as different meaning possibilities within this one function as in Figure 3.1.

Figure 3.1

Function		Meaning option		Realisation
		reaction	＼	[gaɪ gaɪ gaɪ]
Personal	utterance			
		curiosity	＼	[ga]

Figure 3.1 is to be read as saying that any utterance interpreted as fulfilling the personal function will have one of two meanings, either a 'reaction' or a 'curiosity' meaning. If the former, then the meaning is expressed by [gaɪ gaɪ gaɪ], if the latter, then by [ga].

Of the other signs, 4, [amamama], is distinctive in being used as a means of getting things, while 1(b), the forceful version of [ga], and 3, the greeting [x:], are related to each other in that both serve to initiate an occasion of sharing or togetherness. Thus the protolanguage can be schematised for this stage of development as in Figure 3.2.

If we stop for a moment to consider the uses to which we ourselves put language, and the different meanings we can convey, the list will

11

Figure 3.2   Hal's protolanguage at nine and a half months

Function	Meaning option		Realisation
Instrumental	utterance ————	demand	\ [amamama]
Interactional	utterance —	greet	\ [x:]
		engage	\ [ga] (loud)
Personal	utterance —	reaction	\ [gaɪ gaɪ gaɪ]
		curiosity	\ [ga]

be almost endless. In comparison, the functions of language indicated here for the infant just beginning to use symbols are few, and the meanings given expression are very limited. This is as we would expect of course, but despite this restriction, we can see that the meanings expressed do spread across a range, in that some were more concerned with the world of objects, events, and feelings, while others additionally—or instead—took on more the character of a dialogue, where another person was addressed and generally made some response to the child's vocalisation.

The later protolanguage

In Figure 3.3, we see the way in which this protolanguage had expanded by the time another four months had passed.

Expansion of the linguistic system took the form of additional meaning choices within existing functions, and one additional function where vocalisation accompanied a 'let's pretend' situation, or constituted a kind of play with patterns of sound (and perhaps meaning). By this age, Halliday's son, Nigel, had an even more extensive system of signs (Halliday, 1975), and there are doubtless other children who have produced smaller ones (see Carter, 1979). There will certainly be some variations too in the kinds of occasion that call forth vocalisation in different children.

What we need to consider here are the limitations and possibilities of this kind of linguistic system. With his protolanguage, Hal was able to 'communicate' with his inner circle, cementing relationships and engendering feelings of intimacy. He could express his reactions to the world outside, defining his own personality as he did so. Moreover, he could get what he wanted in the way of refreshments, playthings, attention, and comfort (to the extent that his communications were successful of course).

Perhaps the first question to ask is this: how necessary was it for the child to create a symbol system in order to do all this? It seems to me that in principle an infant could probably do all these things without evolving a protolanguage. But it is difficult to envisage as extensive a set of specific meanings as Hal created—meanings that were related to one another in differing ways—being conveyed without a vocal or gestural symbolic system.

Figure 3.3 Hal's protolanguage at 13½ months

Function	Meaning option				Main realisation	Gloss
Instrumental	u.	require aid			[ʔə] (a grunt)	'somebody do something!'
		demand			[maɪ] ('mah')	'I want that'
Interactional		object mediated	ritual giving		[dɪ] ('dee')	'here you are'
			display		[adʒà] (loud) ('uh-jah')	'see what I'm doing/ see what I've got'
	u.	exchange			raspberry noise; [ʔæ ::ʔæ]('a-a')	'I say—you say'
		share amusement			[æ ::hæ ha] ('hahaha')	'isn't this hilarious?'
		greet			[dàda] (+ smile) (dadda)	'it's you! / you and me!'
Personal		feeling	pleasure	general	[æ] ('a!')	'I like this (you know)'
				taste	[m:::] ('mmmm')	'this tastes good'
			surprise		[ōu] ('oh')	'ooh!'
	u.	interest	general		[gà] ('gah')	'that's interesting'
			specific		[ɹθ] ('t-th')	'an animal—oh, how interesting!'
		activity	general		[gà] ('gah')	'I'm busy (with this)'
			special	achievement	[adʒà] ('ajah')	'managed it!'
				exploration	[adà; adá adá adà]	'I'm busy sorting (contents of) this out'
Imaginative	u.	ride bike			[br:::]	'I'm riding a bike'
		sound play			signs; 'singing', etc.	'tra-la'

Note: u. = utterance

There is a further question to consider here, which is this: if he went on expanding his protolanguage, would he be able to do with it all the things we as adults do with language—to argue, threaten, invite, cajole, denounce, explain, and so on?

some social roles adopted in using the protolanguage

Let us consider the social roles children adopt or impose as protolanguage speakers. They appear to be of the following kind: demander (addressee as supplier) of food or objects; seeker (addressee as provider) of comfort, aid, or attention; expresser of feelings; participant in a game, and the like. And, as I have just suggested, these roles could also be played out non-linguistically.

However, there are many things adults do when they speak that involve them in adopting or assigning roles that can **only** be expressed by means of language. Examples would be those involved in seeking, providing, or disclaiming information; promising; expressing doubt or certainty; and so on. No matter how large a protolinguistic sytem might be, its user could not do with it all or any of these things that we feel are normal for even an immature speaker of language proper.

limitations of the protolanguage

What is the limitation of the protolanguage that prevents it from doing this? The most obvious shortcoming of the system would seem to be that only those in very close contact with the child would have a chance of understanding his or her vocalisations. While this is perfectly true, this restriction of membership of the speech community is not the kind of limitation I have been talking about. To consider the limitation of functional potential, we have to look at the nature of the infant symbol, or sign. Obviously one key limitation here is the apparent lack of representational or experiential content to the sign. By this I mean the child's inability to refer specifically to any 'bit' of outside reality. One cannot query, assert, or deny without some means of referring to things, persons, actions, and the like. A first step towards a more mature language will therefore be the introduction of names into the system.

Before pursuing this point, exactly what is meant by the term 'name' will become clearer if I answer the possible objection that Hal did appear to be able to refer to something specific with one of the signs of his protolanguage at thirteen and a half months. The sign expressed as [ʈθ]—'t-th'—has been glossed as meaning 'an animal—ooh how interesting!'. When we consider this, and other signs too, it is clear that a protolanguage **can** make reference to the real world, but not by means of names. [ʈθ] is not an infant vocabulary item equivalent to *animal* in English or *Tier* in German. This is because its meaning is not simply the experiential one of 'animal', but the whole of 'an animal—ooh how interesting'. In other words, its meaning derives solely from the personal function of reacting to, and expressing curiosity about, the immediate environment. Thus the 'animal' aspect of the meaning cannot be separated out and made available for use on other occasions to mean 'let me have that animal', 'let's play animals', or 'I'm pretending to be an animal'. Indeed it cannot even mean 'that **was** an animal—ooh how interesting!'. So even though a child could go on increasing his or her repertoire of sounds, inventing new ones for each of the above meanings (should he or she wish to express them), it is clear that the limitation of the protolanguage is not essentially one of size, but of kind.

Chapter 4

Phase II—the transition period

For Hal, the first move beyond the protolanguage was the introduction of lexis (mother tongue words) into his linguistic system. His first word was *puss*, and if we look at some typical occasions of use over the four or five weeks when it was his only word, we can see how it is different from a protolinguistic sign, and how its presence changes the potential of the language.

Hal's first word: examples of its use at about 14 months

Example 4.1
Hal and M are visiting friends. H notices a cat and points to it, repeating excitedly *puss*; *puss*; *puss*; *puss*.

Example 4.2
Hal announces *puss* and walks down hall to room where cat is usually to be found.

Example 4.3
[Hal enters kitchen, whimpering]
M: Hm? What are you doing?
H: Puss [pointing back to the door; he leads M into next room]
       Puss; puss; puss
M: Are you looking for her?
H: [Looks at M and points at window sill] Puss; puss
       [M notices cat and lifts Hal to stroke her]

Example 4.4
Hal is standing on sofa pointing at window. Earlier he found and played with the cat on the sill. Now he begins to repeat *puss*; *puss*; *puss* while pointing at the window. M looks out of window, but can't see a cat and says something to this effect. Ten minutes later Hal repeats the scene, pointing and saying *puss*. He then turns to address M, repeating to her *puss*.

Example 4.5
H lifts bathmat and peeps under, saying *puss*; *puss* [imaginatively re-playing real scenes of discovering the cat under bed-clothes, etc.].

If we consider where the word *puss* fits into Hal's existing language system at 14 months, we will have to consider it to be an expression in each of the functions. Examples 4.1 and 4.2 would be personal in function, expressing interest in, and curiosity about, the environment. Utterances in Example 4.3 are instrumental, in Example 4.4, they are personal and interactional, while Example 4.5 is an example of imaginative use.

Even further than this, we can see that the possibilities of the existing functions were immediately extended by the presence of a word in the language. The personal function could now include anticipatory observations or statements of intention as illustrated in Example 4.2. In Example 4.4 the first utterances were perhaps examples of a recalling occasion within the personal function, while the final utterance there concerns **shared** recall of a shared past event, a new possibility within the interactional function. Similarly, the instrumental function had now extended so that Hal could demand a specific thing (the cat), whether or not that desired thing was in shared physical view or had been linguistically offered by another person.

In using *puss*, then, Hal had developed a name, a way of referring to, or representing, a class of objects without being limited to any single functional meaning such as 'I'm interested', 'give me', or 'see with me', and without being limited to talking about the immediate here-and-now situation.

The development of two macrofunctions

At the same time as the first word appeared, it was possible to distinguish two principal intonation contours coming to be used in the proto-language. One or two of the instrumental and interactional signs (see Figure 3.3) were spoken on a high-pitched level tone (or sometimes a rising tone), whereas all the others (personal, imaginative, and most interactional expressions) were articulated with a falling tone.

This development is important as it prefigures the next step towards adult language, which was for Hal to utter *puss*, and other words as he developed them, on one of these two tones, depending on the meaning expressed. Let us take the following examples of small texts as typical of this period (about 17-18 months).

Example 4.6
Without looking at anyone, Hal announces *sòck* and walks over to the sock drawer. Unable to open the drawer he repeats *sōck*; *sōck* ever more frantically, looking round at M.

Example 4.7
Hal is pushing a trolley and when it gets stuck he says *ōh deàr* without looking up. He tries to get it moving again, but fails and says to M *ōh dēar*; *ōh dēar*; M helps him.

Example 4.8
H is looking at a picture book. He points to a dog's tail and says *tàil*. He takes the book over to the cat and sits down pointing at the picture tail and the cat's tail in turn, repeating *tàil* each time.

Obviously we could continue to interpret these utterances in terms of protolinguistic functions, as was done for the *puss* examples. However, an interpretation along these lines will fail to capture the meaning distinction being carried by the intonation. Even from such a small sample, I think it is clear that the distinction is related to one of monologue vs. dialogue, since the high level tone was usually addressed to another person, while the falling tone generally appeared to be self-addressed. Further than this, we can say that the level tone characterises an active, demanding kind of speech act, while the falling tone is something more like a reflective comment.

So although individual protolanguage functions can still be pointed to, the linguistic system has now organised itself in terms of only two more general functions. These Halliday has termed MACROFUNCTIONS in order to emphasise both their broader scope and the fact that they can be recognised on linguistic, and not only contextual, grounds.

Mathetic macrofunction—language for learning

Halliday has suggested the term MATHETIC for the use of language in the commenting mode. This term suggests that the function of utterances of this kind is a learning one. The child is using language as a means of understanding the world about him or her. In order to clarify this point, it is obviously necessary to raise the following question: what does it mean to learn through language when you are one and a half to two years old? We can get some insight into this by looking at the various things Hal used his mathetic language to do.

Classification by naming

One thing all children do at this stage is to use language to categorise things. In Example 4.8, we saw Hal comparing a real tail and a symbolic (pictorial) one, not only exploring the provenance of a name, but using the name to sort out related phenomena. Later he would produce more complex forms serving the same purpose, as in Example 4.9.

Example 4.9
H: Mùmmys coffee [pointing at M's cup];
       Dàddys coffee [pointing at F's cup]

And often the adult would ask pseudo-questions to make this naming procedure more interactive, as in Example 4.10.

Example 4.10
[Hal enters flourishing a book]
M: What've you got there?
H: Bòok

On occasions, he also seemed to be working out the relation of parts to a whole in his classifying speech, as when he would label a whole and then a series of parts, as in Example 4.11.

18

Example 4.11

(a) H: Dòg; lèg; tàil

(b) H: Càr; light; whèel

Running commentary

More complex phenomena were also given a verbal interpretation. For example, on one occasion when a slamming noise was heard, Hal could be seen to be making sense of the occurrence within the pattern of his experience, as in Example 4.12.

Example 4.12

H: Bàng; dòor; dàdda

Later, observations of his own or other people's behaviour were verbalised in structural forms, but with the same kind of function, as in Example 4.13.

Example 4.13

H: [watching F] Daddy putting slippers òn

Statement of intention

Processing instructions

In Example 4.6, we saw Hal verbalising an immediate intention, the first beginnings of using language to formulate a plan of action. A later example at 20 months (Example 4.14) shows him doing this as a by-product of processing an instruction given him.

Example 4.14

[Hal is playing inside with a flower from the garden]

H: Flòwer; flòwer, flòwer; flòwer [as he pulls the petals off onto chair]

M: Oh, Hal, you do make a mess

H: Mèss; mèss; mèss; mèss [rubs at petal stuck on his hands] tōwel; tōwel [runs off to bathroom to get one, but all are in wash, returns to M] tōwel

M: In your bedroom, Hal. There's a white towel there. In the bedroom.

H: [to himself] Bèdroom; tòwel [runs off to M's bedroom. Returns with pair of towelling shorts. Rubs at petals] nàughty; nàughty; nàughty; mèss

Anticipation and recall

In Example 4.3, we saw Hal referring to a past event. In Example 4.15, it is clear that the past situation is being brought to bear in order to predict or anticipate what will be the case—all part of finding patterns in experience.

Example 4.15

Hal reaches a finger gingerly to a light bulb and says *hòt*; *hòt*

There are also many examples where Hal recounts to himself a past experience as if to reconsider it and make sense of it.

19

Example 4.16

Hal has been smacked for picking a prize flower after being warned not to. After he calms down, he says *nàughty; nàughty; sèe; flòwer; nàughty; bàng* [= the smack] *bàdboy*

Example 4.17

[Hal is wrenching about the feet of a new wind-up duck]
M: No, no. Don't do that, Hal, no, no, no, no, no. It'll get broken.
H: Nò, nò. Bròken. Nò [eventually gives toy to M]
[That evening and for the rest of the week when bathing with same duck, H repeats the wrenching action and says again *nò, nò, bròken*, looking at the toy.]

Speaker/hearer relations in mathetic speech

As we have seen, the child may be concerned with sorting out social norms (picking flowers is forbidden; destroying them inside constitutes mess to be cleaned up), as well as interpretations of material ones (relations of cause and effect, etc.—don't do this because it will end up broken; last time I touched this it was hot). None the less, it is striking that his speech generally appears to be directed at himself rather than at any addressee. Piaget's term 'egocentric speech' is perhaps most useful as a characterisation of mathetic language of this kind, since even when the child is apparently engaging in dialogue, mathetic speech has this 'private' character. When Hal responded with *bèdroom; tòwel* in Example 4.14, he was not acknowledging the addressee's statement as in a comparable adult dialogue, such as the following:

A: There's a towel in the bedroom
B: In the bedroom, right

I make this claim on the grounds that in such situations eye-contact with an addressee was most often not established by Hal, and mathetic utterances were often spoken very quietly. Moreover, there were frequent dialogues of the following kind (see Example 4.18).

Example 4.18

[Hal is taking things off the bedside table]
M: What have you got there?
H: Wàtch [handing it over]; pèn [handing it over]; glàsses; còffee; all-gòne [peering into a cup]; còffee; all-gòne; còffee
M: What does this watch say? [holding it up to him]
H: Glasses [handing them over]
M: Mummy's glasses. [taking them]

Even at the protolinguistic stage, child and adult take turns in speaking, but in other respects, exchanges like that above are not really comparable with adult dialogue. It is always up to the adult to ask the 'question' to which the child's utterance (which is probably coming anyway) will make a relevant 'response' (see Example 4.10), and to acknowledge the child's remarks, as above, even if the compliment is not returned.

Mathetic speech—an instrument of learning

The mathetic function is not to be interpreted as the function of learning language. While the language used to, and around, children is part of the reality they are making sense of at this stage, it is also the tool with which they discover and impose patterns on their experience of everything else. There is thus a symbiotic relationship between learning about reality and learning the language—each is a consequence of the other. And it is surely the combination of learning language and learning about the world that provides the greatest impetus for the speed with which children make progress in their mother tongue.

There is a close relationship between learning about reality and learning language.

Pragmatic macrofunction—language as action

Although I have suggested that the term 'egocentric speech' may have some validity as a characterisation of mathetic speech at this time, it would be quite wrong to assume that the child therefore has nothing in the way of 'social' speech. As we would expect from the range of functions present at the protolinguistic stage, Hal also continued to use language as a prime means of interacting with others. This was one of the chief characteristics of utterances spoken on a level or rising tone.

When using level tone utterances, Hal was always aiming to achieve some definite result, usually the attainment of goods and services. In the nature of things it was usually up to someone else to fulfill his demands, so these utterances occurred in genuinely interactive situations. However, **linguistic** interaction was not the goal. Halliday has suggested the term PRAGMATIC for this use of language to get things done. Some examples will give the main kinds of demands made by Hal at around 18 months (see Examples 4.19–4.22).

Demands for goods

Example 4.19
[At breakfast table]
H: Tōast; tōast; tōast [looking around at F at toaster]
F: Toast?
H: Tōast; Tóast; m̀
[F brings toast to table]
H: Tōast; tōast
F: [Buttering it] Yes, toast is coming.
H: Tōast; dāddā

Here we can see that neither the offer implied in bringing the toast to the table, nor the verbal reassurance that he can have it, satisfies Hal.

Accomplish task (I do)

Example 4.20
H: [looking at switch, then M] Līght; līght
M: [lifts him up] Oh, all right.

21

Notice that in this case if M had switched the light on, Hal would have been infuriated, not appeased.

Control other (You do)

Example 4.21

H: Clāp; clāp [to F who isn't joining in music session]
     [F complies]

Achieve interaction (Be with me)

Example 4.22

[M returns home without F]
H: Dāddā [looking round for F]
M: Oh, looking for Daddy? He's coming later . . .

It can be seen that pragmatic speech was entirely related to here-and-now situations, although it was now possible for Hal to request something that was not present, as in the last example.

The nature of the transition

Halliday characterises this stage of development as transitional, because the language system is in some ways like the protolanguage and in other respects like an adult metafunctional system. It may seem as though one aspect of development constitutes a limitation, in that the entry into the mother tongue apparently heralds a reduction in the number of functions that language serves for the child. But this is of course not the case. Hal could still express meanings in all the functions that were originally identified, and a few more besides, as well as increasing the scope of the original functions. There will always be more and more individual uses of language in his life. What has happened, though, is that only two more broadly conceived functions, which therefore may be termed macrofunctions, have been coded into the language system by means of the tone contrast.

In other words, Hal could now say *pūss* or *pùss*; *clāp* or *clàp*, and one kind of meaning—**experiential** meaning—the thing or action referred to—was expressed by the choice of word; and another kind of meaning—**interpersonal** meaning—was expressed by means of tone. Thus Hal was able to express the two kinds of meaning in a single utterance even at the one-word stage. His linguistic system could therefore be represented as an integrated set of resources with two components as in Figure 4.1.

Figure 4.1 indicates that any of four options for 'aspect of experience' can be chosen **and** either of two choices of 'speech function'. 'Aspect of experience' options are expressed (or realised) by a lexical item while each 'speech function' option is expressed by a particular tone. Thus any utterance embodies more than one kind of meaning option and consists of more than one expression form.

Figure 4.1 A transition linguistic system showing its resemblance to adult language

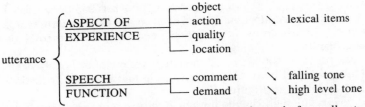

```
                          ┌── object
           ┌ ASPECT OF    ├── action        ╲  lexical items
           │ EXPERIENCE   ├── quality
           │              └── location
utterance ─┤
           │
           │ SPEECH       ┌── comment        ╲  falling tone
           └ FUNCTION     └── demand         ╲  high level tone
```

Note: ⎰ indicates that choices are simultaneously made from all sets of
       ⎱ meaning options enclosed by it
       ╲ means 'is realised by'

However, there are a number of ways in which the language was still similar to that of the protolinguistic phase. One important fact is that despite developing this facility for encoding an experiential meaning, together with a choice of speech act meaning, Hal did not greatly exploit this at first. Only about a quarter of his vocabulary

Figure 4.2   A transition linguistic system showing its resemblance to the protolanguage

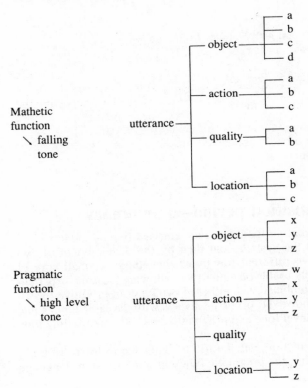

occurred in the two possible modes. For the rest, some words were used solely in the pragmatic macrofunction, and a rather larger set were used only in the mathetic macrofunction. There were thus two largely separate lexical repertoires, just as separate symbol sets had been created for each protolanguage function. Indeed he even had two different words for *Mummy* : [mʌ̀ɪ]—'muy' on mathetic occasions and [māmā] on pragmatic ones.

All this suggests that instead of one integrated metafunctional system of the kind given in Figure 4.1, there were in fact two largely distinct languages as shown in Figure 4.2.

Moreover, although Hal did initiate linguistic exchanges (as indeed he did at the protolinguistic stage), he could adopt only one of two interpersonal roles, neither of which was a fully fledged speech role. I say this because his 'comment' was not directed to an addressee, thus requiring a linguistic acknowledgment. On the other hand, his interactive 'demand' imposed only a non-linguistic role on the addressee, that of provider of goods and services, help, or company.

the failure of some early attempts to elicit information from Hal

It should be added that although some comments did appear to take the form of appropriate responses to *What's that?*, *Where's the X?* kinds of questions (see Example 4.10), a genuine information-seeking inquiry was usually simply not responded to. The following unsuccessful dialogue was typical of attempts to elicit information in the period 18–22 months, when the inquirer genuinely sought to find out something.

Example 4.23
[Hal has eaten his meal with F. Later M arrives home]
M: What did you have for tea?
H: [silence]
M: What did you have for tea, darling?
H: Tea
M: Yes, what did you have for tea?
H: [silence]
M: Did you have an egg?
H: Egg
M: And some toast?
H: [silence]

The early transition period—a summary

The move into the mother tongue is characterised first by the introduction of names into the system, and then by the development of two tones conveying two different functional meanings. A small core of vocabulary was freely usable on either tone, allowing the same experiential meaning to be combined with either of two kinds of primitive speech role. Most names, however, occurred always with the same tone; some being restricted to level tone and pragmatic uses, others to falling tone and mathetic uses.

The mathetic function was the use of language to learn, to build up a picture of reality; the pragmatic function was the use of language

24

to act on that reality. Mathetic speech was largely self-addressed and where it occurred in dialogue, it did not ever serve to convey information unknown to the addressee. Pragmatic language generally served to initiate a dialogue, but this was incidental to achieving a material response from the addressee.

Chapter 5

From Phase II to Phase III

As we have seen, utterances of the early transition tended to be concerned **either** with experiential content (mathetic speech) **or** with interaction with another person (pragmatic speech).

New developments

I propose now to select just a few samples of Hal's speech produced after 18 months of age, with a view to illustrating how both experiential and interpersonal aspects gradually began to carry equal weight.

Mathetic speech

Example 5.1
M has told H off for pulling the cat's tail
A few minutes later H addresses F in another room, and says *tàil*; *tàil*; *tàil*; *pùssy*; *tàil*; *pùssy*; *tàil*; *pùssy*; *bàdboy*

Example 5.2
H: Hòrsey [pointing at sheep in book]
M: That's not a horse; it's a sheep!
H: Hòrsey!
M: No, it's a sheep.
H: Hòrse!
M: Sheep, baa-aa . . .

Example 5.3
H: Bòy [pointing at girl in book]
M: It's a girl.
H: Bòy; bòy
M: It's a girl.
H: Bòy; bòy
M: It's not; it's a girl.
H: Bòy; bōy [anxiously]
M: All right; it's a boy with long hair and a skirt.

In what way can the above texts be regarded as showing evidence of fresh development? The importance of Example 5.1 is that it is an early example of Hal adopting the role of giver of information. From the beginning of the mother tongue period (see Example 4.4), he had used language to tell over with someone some aspect of shared experience. But the potential of language actually to create the experience for someone who had not shared it is an understanding the child arrives at more slowly. And in Hal's case, between 18 and 20 months, almost every rare example of information giving was an immediate recount of this kind, reworking some heart-felt occasion of reprimand and misbehaviour. Moreover he still could not respond to information-seeking questions addressed to him, where he was asked to recreate something for the interlocutor's benefit, rather than for his own spontaneously felt need to reconsider some significant event by retelling it. Hal adopts the role of giving information.

Examples 5.2 and 5.3, in comparison with other cases where adult and child classify objects together, show Hal engaging in argumentation, either to make a joke or in all seriousness.

Thus, the new things that Hal can do within the mathetic function are all important in that they make the representation of experiential content something that occurs in an interaction where roles of speaking are adopted or assigned.

Pragmatic speech

New pragmatic developments are illustrated in the following examples.

Example 5.4
H: [taking a sprout] Eàt
[looks at M] Eát
M: No.
[H places it on table instead]

Example 5.5
[M & H are out. The beach is to one side of them, the park on the other]
M: Where do you want to go?
H: Beàch. Go on bēach

In Example 5.4, we see Hal accepting, indeed seeking, a linguistic rather than a material response to a pragmatic request. In Example 5.5, we see him accepting an offer by giving information. Demands made in immediate response to an adult offer began to take a falling tone at about 20 months. This is either because the position of the utterance in the exchange marked it sufficiently as a demand, or because the experiential content of the response was being foregrounded. In either case, Hal was showing a sensitivity to the fact that these are linguistic exchanges as well as exchanges of goods and services, and that they are concerned both with speech roles and representational content.

Finally, you probably noticed that the final utterance from Hal in Example 5.3 was also a pragmatic one—judging from its tone. It was one of a very few examples where the notion of demand was

perhaps being generalised to include the demand for information—
'isn't it *boy*?'. (This is of interest because this was the route by which
Halliday's son, Nigel, came to information-seeking.)

What we have seen in the new developments outlined above
amounts to a blurring of the mathetic/pragmatic distinction in certain
cases. Mathetic utterances were no longer purely reflective and concerned with experiential matters. Now, on some occasions at least,
linguistic interaction was required. At the same time, not all pragmatic
utterances were purely active in the sense of demanding goods and
services directly. The action required might now be a linguistic action,
and the demand itself might involve representing some aspect of reality.
The formal reflexes of these changes were a freeing from functional
restriction of the vocabulary (though many new structures were limited
to one or other macrofunction for a time) and the beginning of a change
in the intonation system.

Into a metafunctional system—the final step

The story of the transition into the mother tongue is a paradoxical one.
The first milestone involves the creation of the mathetic/pragmatic
distinction. This step of generalising protolanguage uses into two broader
functions provides a strategy for building up experiential and
interpersonal meaning choices. However, these cannot come to be
expressed simultaneously, and with equal status given to each kind of
meaning in any utterance, until the distinction is lost, and every utterance
is **both** reflective **and** interactive.

the development of
the English mood
system

Hal's final step was to develop the English MOOD SYSTEM, which
is the interpersonal system in the grammar that expresses the status of
an utterance as an interaction with another speaker: a declarative is the
typical grammatical form for giving information, an interrogative for
demanding information, and an imperative for expressing a command.
At the same time, Hal had to abandon his two-way tone system, which
was inadequate for the more complex set of roles involved in fully fledged
exchanges of information and goods and services.

When Hal first produced a Wh- form it was on occasions like the
following at about 22 months (see Examples 5.6 and 5.7).

Example 5.6
H & M are playing with a posting box.
H looks in and says *whats in-there; whats in-there; peg*

Example 5.7
H finds a hair in the bath and holds it up to M saying *whats this; hair*

Here he was not seeking information from another person when
he used the interrogative form. What then **was** he doing? I think we
can say that he was demonstrating his recognition of the form as an
information-demanding one, and when his hitherto relatively non-
interactive mathetic comment (*peg* or *hair*) was embedded in a question-

28

response sequence of this sort, it became marked as an information giver. What I would suggest that Hal was doing here was playing the roles of both information seeker and answerer, as a preliminary to engaging in genuine interactional dialogue to exchange information.

Of course, it could be argued that he was simply using *whats that* to focus the addressee's attention, as a kind of 'Hey' or 'Look' introduction to a remark. But Hal's next move was to enlist the adult partner's help in creating little conversational exchanges that served to mark the speech act status of his 'part'. Consider Examples 5.8-5.10

Example 5.8
[H is pinching himself and looking up into M's face]
H: Dont hurt yourself
M: Yes indeed, don't hurt yourself, silly.
[H grins and releases himself]

Example 5.9
F: What's the matter?
H: Bump finger
   [looks intently at F] This finger
F: Oh, was it this finger?
H: This finger

Example 5.10
[H had fussed earlier about finding and putting on his slippers. Now he approaches M without them]
H: [looking into M's face closely] What happened [ə] slippers?
M: [recognising her cue] Oh, what happened to your slippers?
H: [delighted] Take [ə] slippers off!

In the first case, Example 5.8, Hal wanted his non-verbal action of releasing his leg to be part of a sequence of imperative command followed by non-verbal compliance. In the second, Example 5.9, he wanted to tell F which finger hurt, but wanted the status of his information to be clearly marked by following the appropriate question. Similarly, in Example 5.10, he wanted to tell his mother something, but wanted his utterance to occur as part of a dialogue, where his speech role would be unmistakable.

For Hal, this kind of discourse, where mathetic and pragmatic were brought together by the embedding of references to reality (the mathetic norm) into a context of dialogue (more typical of the pragmatic), sees him on the brink of an adult-like metafunctional system. Once he moved into using the mood forms in a genuine interaction—i.e. actually seeking information with *Whats that?* and giving others commands with imperatives, and freely giving information on request, he can be said to have a set of interpersonal mood choices co-existing with a set of experiential choices.

His mood system was not expressed exactly as in adult English, but he had, by two years of age, a set of interpersonal meaning options each with a specific linguistic realisation (see Figure 5.1).

See Chapter 2.

29

Figure 5.1 Outline of general interpersonal options

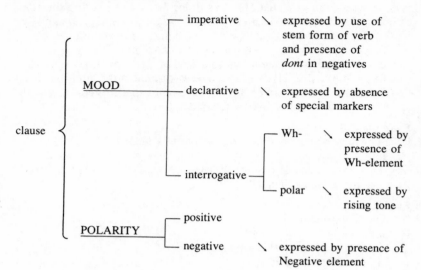

A 'polar'
interrogative requires
a yes or no
response, e.g. *Did
he come?*

      Figure 5.1 shows that any clause spoken by Hal could be formally
recognised as being of one of three mood types and one of two polarity
types. In addition, he had, for any clause, a set of experiential meaning
options expressed by TRANSITIVITY structures, such as Actor + Process
(+ Goal) (+ Circumstance of time or location). These were of the kind
outlined in Figure 5.2, and could be mapped on to the structures produced
by the interpersonal choices.

Figure 5.2 Outline of general experiential options

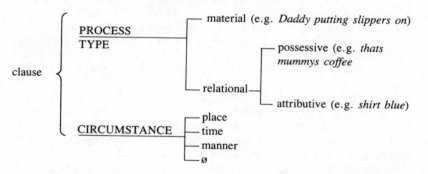

The grammar as a whole can be represented as one complete system as in Figure 5.3.

Figure 5.3 A Phase III grammar

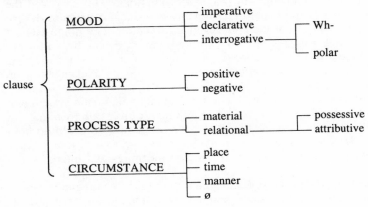

Figure 5.3 shows that the speaker has four co-existing sets of linguistic options (known technically as systems). Two of these systems are interpersonal in nature (those of mood and polarity), and the other two are experiential in nature (those of process type and circumstance, jointly known as transitivity).

If the language were represented in greater detail, polarity options would be found to interrelate most closely with mood ones (when tags are included in the description, for example), without affecting transitivity choices. This is what is meant by grouping them as a component—the interpersonal component—of the grammar.

Finally, it should be said that virtually as soon as Hal was able to map mood choices onto transitivity choices in a single utterance form, he showed some ability to choose an 'incongruent' mood form: one that did not match the speech act being expressed. The first example was the use of the declarative (i.e. information-giving) mood form—*thats mine* or *thats Hals*—to express what was in fact a command to leave something alone. (Its status as a command was demonstrated by the fact that acknowledging the information with *Yes, it is yours* was not an acceptable response.)

The capacity to choose an 'incongruent' mood form develops.

This phenomenon is sometimes referred to as the use of 'indirect speech acts', and is one means we all have of enriching the potential of our linguistic resources. In effect it meant that Hal was beginning to build up two distinct sets of interpersonal options: one was a set of speech role choices (giving/demanding/acknowledging information and goods and services) and the other was the set of mood options that expressed them, but not always in the same way.

Entry into Phase III—a brief summary

Developments in the later transition period concerned the bringing together of the mathetic and pragmatic functions. This involved the freeing of words and structures from any functional restriction. It also meant the evolution of the concept of information. The pragmatic act of demanding was extended in a limited way to demanding information and other linguistic responses, and Hal learnt to embed the mathetic representation of experiential content into dialogue exchanges of an informative kind.

At the beginning of the transition, Hal had a linguistic system that by and large allowed him **either** to talk about things **or** to engage in talk with other people. At the end of the transition, he could do both at once. He had developed resources for making two different kinds of meanings simultaneously (experiential meanings and interpersonal ones).

The move from the protolanguage to the mother tongue is one in which the notion of function is gradually built into the language system. Protolanguage utterances can be interpreted as fulfilling one of a small number of uses of language. These uses (instrumental, personal, etc.) are inferred by the hearer (or researcher) from non-linguistic situational and behavioural clues. During the transition, these infant functions are subsumed by two more generalised uses—language for learning and language as action. The development of a partially distinct set of words and a specific tone for each function is evidence for this development. Moreover, when either tone could be used with the same set of words (and later, structures) depending on the macrofunctional meaning conveyed, we have evidence for this broad functional contrast being coded into the language system itself.

Finally, as described in the previous section, these two functions come to be served simultaneously by all utterances. The macrofunctions may then be said to have evolved into metafunctions: very general uses of language in terms of which the meaning options of the language are organised. Metafunctions are thus components of the language system that reflect the fundamental uses of language.

Chapter 6

Overview: the development of language as a changing relation between speech and context

Context in the protolanguage

The development of the mother tongue is the story of the child's changing view of the context for speech. During the protolanguage, the child produces symbolic vocalisations in a limited range of contexts. I have been interpreting these in functional terms, as uses of language (instrumental, interactional, and so on). Alternatively, one could conceive of the contexts as opposing object-oriented to person-oriented meanings, or ranged on a continuum from self-expressive to outward directed meanings.

Context in the transition

The importance of the intonation contrast of the early transition period, however, is that it provides some linguistic evidence that the child is now interpreting any context for speech as of one of two kinds: either one for reflecting on the world, or one for intruding upon the world. When Hal said *bàdboy* recalling a misdeed, or *deer got àntler* pointing to a picture, or *bring wàter* on his way to fulfilling a command to do so, he was characterising the context for speech as a reflective one where he sorted out experience with the aid of language. When he said *bāll* reaching for a ball, or *pōrridge; sēē* requesting a lift, or *play mīaōw* seeking a game, he was characterising the context for speech as an active one, one where he intruded himself onto reality.

This is of course to idealise the situation to some extent. When Hal said *pōrridge*, he was certainly interpreting the context as an active one, given that he used a high level tone and a word restricted to pragmatic uses. But none the less, he did use a vocabulary item and thus was also incidentally classifying the desired object.

Developments during the transition involve the child in moving away from this interpretation of contexts for speech as **either** reflective **or** active. We have seen how some mathetic contexts became more active, in the sense of interactive, with the advent of argument, jokes,

The transition language is used for reflecting upon the world or for intruding upon the world.

and restricted information giving. On the other hand, pragmatic contexts became more reflective in that more things, events, places, etc. were referred to in the process of making a demand (with a falling tone for responses marking the increased prominence of the experiential aspect). Moreover, we have seen here the beginnings of the use of pragmatic language to learn, as in permission requests (establishing social norms), and the rare requests for a name.

At this stage we can say that contexts for speech were being interpreted by the child as having two unequal aspects—one concerned with the things talked about, and the other with speaker/hearer relations. The tone used indicated which aspect was dominant in any particular case..

Context in Phase III

By the time Hal learned the grammatical system of mood, his original two-way tone distinction had virtually disappeared, since the contextual distinction it was signalling had disappeared also. By this time almost all utterances equally made reference to the real world and signalled a specific interactional status for the speaker (and thus the hearer). When this was the case, the child can be taken as construing the context in terms of two component aspects, neither of which took precedence over the other.

Field and tenor are discussed in some detail in *Language, Context, and Text* (Halliday & Hasan, 1989).

These two components of the situation have been termed within systemic theory FIELD and TENOR. Field consists of the activity taking place with which the language is concerned and the things talked about. Tenor refers to relations between the speaker and hearer. Let us look in these terms at a very brief and simple fragment of a dialogue in which Hal participated when he was two years old.

Example 6.1

H: Thats blùe [pointing at blue peg]
M: Yes, that's blue.
H: Thats blùe [pointing to another]
M: No.
H: Thats blùe [pointing at orange one]; thats òrange
M: That's orange [agreeing].
H: Thats blùe [pointing at another peg]
M: No.
H: Thats blùe [pointing at blue one]
M: Yes.
H: Thats blùe [pointing at another]
M: No.
H: Thats blùe
M: No.
H: Thats órange
M: Yes.
H: Thats òrange

Field determines choice of lexis.

In this exchange we can see that the field—a naming game in relation to a board of coloured pegs—determines the set of lexical items

34

used: a choice of two from a repertoire of four of five in Hal's case. It also determines the choice of an attributive clause type (*That's X*).

The tenor component of the speech situation has mother and child in an unequal relation; mother is the source of expertise *vis-à-vis* this field, while Hal is the novice testing his hypotheses against her knowledge. This determines the mood and polarity of the utterances chosen.

One other point about the dialogue is that without the 'stage directions', we would not now know exactly what was being talked about, because the pegs are not named. The reason is obvious: the referent of *that* was in each case clearly visible to both parties and could be physically indicated by pointing. The presence of such deictic reference items is not determined by field or tenor, but by a third component of the situation known as MODE. Mode refers to the role the language itself plays in the encounter, which is something that depends partly on the physical distance between the interlocutors. A face-to-face ongoing interaction will typically give rise to linguistic inexplicitness of the kind we find here.

Mode refers to the role of language in the interaction; it is discussed in *Language, Context, and Text* (Halliday & Hasan, 1989).

The reason that the mode aspect of the context of situation has not been brought up earlier is that my description of Hal's language development has focused throughout on the development of the experiential and interpersonal metafunctions, and the corresponding two components of the CONTEXT OF SITUATION: field and tenor. But in order to create coherent discourses, the child was also developing the textual metafunction through which mode is expressed. The following fragments of dialogue at two years of age indicate his abilities here. See Halliday (1979) for a more detailed sketch of the development of the textual area of language.

The term 'context of situation' was originally coined by Malinowski in 1923; it is discussed in *Language, Context, and Text* (Halliday & Hasan, 1989).

Example 6.2
F: Put the drink down there [indicating the table].
H: Put it on the <u>new</u> table [choosing a different, new table]

Example 6.3
M: I'm going inside.
H: Hal go inside, too

Example 6.4
M: No, Daddy's a bit tired, now.
H: <u>Mummy</u> do it [= in that case]

He was able to mark by intonational prominence the 'new' information in a clause (shown here by underlining), could use anaphoric reference (the *it* of Example 6.2 refers back to *drink*) and he could implicitly (Example 6.4) or explicitly (with *too* in Example 6.3) link an utterance with one that went before.

The consideration of the context of situation and its relation to discourse is known in linguistics as REGISTER, and I will discuss it in greater detail in Chapter 8 when I will suggest that it provides a way of considering later language development.

Register is discussed in *Language, Context, and Text* (Halliday & Hasan, 1989).

In brief then, the development of a metafunctionally organised linguistic system is also the development by the speaker of a different way of relating speech and context. At the protolanguage stage, a context for speech is one of a small number of ways of behaving that are relevant to the infant's life.

During the early transition, the child begins to interpret the context more abstractly, and to develop a language for each of two different kinds of context. At this stage his or her interpretation of a context for speech does not match that of the adult, as can be illustrated on occasions where misinterpretations arise. Example 6.5 provides such an illustration.

Example 6.5

[Grandmother and Hal are looking at a picture book and naming things. They come to a page of food items]
GM: What's that? [pointing at picture of egg]
H: [turns page]
 Bàll [pointing at picture of ball]
GM: [turns back] There's a biscuit.
H: Bȋkkiē [running into the kitchen]

On this occasion, GM assumed she was still playing the naming game, whereas Hal interpreted her labelling of a biscuit as an offer, because at that time food names were only expressions of pragmatic meaning within his own system. At 18 months, he never labelled food items in his books, and when GM persisted in trying to get him to do so, he understood the context to have switched from a mathetic to a pragmatic one.

Gradually the child comes to bring the two kinds of context together (and his two 'languages' together), until all speech situations are alike interpreted as having component aspects (field, tenor, and mode) expressed by corresponding component areas of the grammar: the experiential, interpersonal, and textual metafunctions.

Throughout the language development process, the child has been (unconsciously) learning to interpret contexts of situation as abstract, symbolic constructs of field, tenor, and mode. And of course, every instance of language he or she has ever had addressed **to** him or her is similarly expressing field, tenor, and mode options through corresponding components of the grammar, and is in this way transparently related to the context. Language addressed to the child is thus well structured, not just in the sense that each utterance provides a model of a well-formed syntactic structure, but in the sense that each utterance plays its part in reflecting the context of situation. This is why the child learns from participating in linguistic interactions what he or she would not learn from a continuous tape recording illustrating all the sound and syntactic structures of the language. It is the nature of language—its metafunctional organisation—and the relation of instances of language use to the context of situation that makes the mother tongue accessible to the infant, although as we have seen there are several stages on the route from protolanguage to Phase III (see Figure 6.1).

Figure 6.1 The changing nature of the context

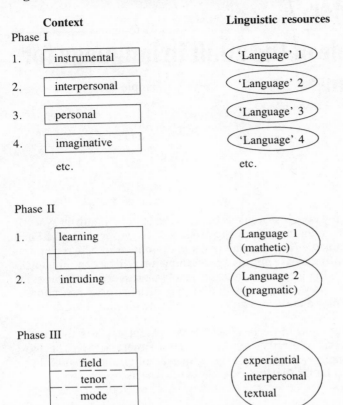

Context   Linguistic resources

Phase I

1. instrumental   'Language' 1
2. interpersonal   'Language' 2
3. personal   'Language' 3
4. imaginative   'Language' 4

    etc.   etc.

Phase II

1. learning   Language 1 (mathetic)
2. intruding   Language 2 (pragmatic)

Phase III

field / tenor / mode   experiential / interpersonal / textual

Chapter 7

The role of the adult in language for learning

Using Language in the Classroom (Lemke, 1989)

The focus of my own research has been on the child's linguistic system, and thus on the utterances he or she produced. However, in educational contexts, I think the role the adult plays in discourses in which children participate when they are engaged in learning has to be a central interest as well. You will come across this in the classroom context in another book in this series. Here, I would simply like to give my impressions concerning one or two aspects of the role of adult speech in the early years.

There are some respects in which the parent appears to take on a conversational role rather similar to that of the teacher. The most obvious example is the use of pseudo questions to allow the child to rehearse what he or she knows.

Example 7.1
[M & H (aged 19 months) are reading]
M: What's this Hal?
H: Bunny
M: Yes; bunny's sleeping.

The child learns from these continually repeated exchanges not just the classification being rehearsed, and the pseudo question-response-evaluation form of 'tutorial' exchange, but also ways of building up longer texts. And this is done in other ways too, particularly by the adult prompting the child to produce satisfactory information-giving texts. This generally depends on some shared knowledge in fact. Consider the following two examples when Hal was 25 months old.

Example 7.2
[F has told M of an incident at the shops, H enters]
M: What did you do at the shops?
H: Jug
M: Jug! What did you do with the jug?
H: Break it
M: You broke the jug!
   And was Daddy cross with you?
H: [slowly grinning] Ye-es!

Example 7.3
M: Tell Daddy where you went today.
F: What did you do today?
H: Feed the birdies
F: Where did you go?
H: [silence]
M: Did you go to the park?
H: No
F: Where did you go?
H: On the beach
F: Did you go in the sea?
H: Yes, wash handies in the water

Although we were unconscious of doing this at the time, our inquisitions of this kind were continually prompting Hal to extend his responses into something that would approach a narrative account, by requiring further specification of events, or details of location or reactions of participants, etc. And it is being a member of the child's inner circle that enables the parent to ask the most appropriate questions, and thus to allow the child to build up a more substantial account jointly with the adult.

Dialogue with an adult encourages the child to provide informative texts.

As teachers, you need to be sensitive to those occasions when adults or children in school engage in discourse that may be different from the children's previous experience. This may simply be the new interactional constraints of a one-to-many conversation compared with the one-to-one situation that the children are familiar with at home. Or it may be the requirement to produce self-sustained discourse without the support of the conversational prompting of parent–child dialogue.

The teaching role adopted by the adult in these examples is unconscious, and what is being taught is not made explicit to either party. My impression is that children in our culture are given most explicit information about what things are, how and why things work, and how to do things physically, and so on. The following fragments of conversation between parent and Hal at two years are typical of this style.

Example 7.4
[F & H are playing with bricks]
F: We're gonna make a bus garage.
H: Giraffe garage. This one's a giraffe garage
F: Giraffes don't have garages, darling. Giraffes don't live in garages. Garages are only for cars.

Example 7.5
[M & H are doing a jigsaw]
M: No, not on the back; that way. You see that bit, you have to put the little knob in the little hole. Can you do that?
[H slots in the piece]
There; that's right!

Example 7.6
H: Oh, what's Mummy doing there [seeing M with vacuum]
M: All right. Press the button.
[H touches it with finger]

M: Hard.
   [H tries to press the button by placing his palm on it]
M: No; with your finger. Press hard with your finger.
   [H does so and succeeds]

I suspect that in our culture it is common for these kinds of matters to receive explicit linguistic explanation. As far as interpersonal relations are concerned, I suspect that only transparent areas of good manners are explicated in adult speech to children—when and how to greet others, the inviolability of other people's property, the (conflicting!) desirability of sharing one's own possessions, etc. Whereas other matters—how to join in an ongoing interaction, how to make satisfactory informative responses, what the relationships are between the various adults in a child's life, and how it is appropriate to name and behave with them—may all be left for the child to infer without any explicit tuition.

One can conceive of things being quite different in other cultures. There it may be taken for granted that a child will 'pick up' the more material aspects of experience and need explicit tuition in forms of address, rights of speaking, and kinship relations. And it is because so much of the child's reality is built up in this implicit way that he or she (and we) can hold conflicting, co-existing views of it. To take one example, Hal during his early years was continually hearing remarks (*She's lovely and soft, isn't she? Mind her tail! Does she want some milk?*), which taken together convey a picture of animals as creatures to admire, with rights to be respected and needs to be taken account of.

No such view of the animal world was ever expressed in such terms, however, and if it had been, there might have been a conflict apparent with an alternative view of animals as a source of food, which was also being endorsed at meals and in conversations accompanying them.

Most of the world view that the child builds up at home through linguistic interaction is conveyed by language that does not set out to teach the child at all, and you may come to consider that this is true even of language used in deliberately pedagogic situations.

Chapter 8

The child entering school—language achievements and limitations

Now that we have looked at one child's actual language-learning experience in the first few years of life, I would like to use that description as a basis for considering general questions relevant to you, who as teachers assume a large measure of responsibility for later language development.

Let us go back to my very first query: has the child mastered his or her language by the age of five? When the answer to this has been 'yes', the school's task has probably been conceived of as one of teaching two new 'translation' skills—those of reading and writing—and then of focusing on things other than language. When the answer has been 'no', the typical reaction has been to look for deficiencies, bits of the language system that the child lacks, or rules that the child has apparently not mastered, and to try to fill the gap or teach the rule.

I hope that the description of language development I have given will allow the question to be considered in a different light, so that the answer we come up with is both 'yes' **and** 'no'.

Has the child mastered his or her mother tongue at age five?

Language achievements

The child **has** mastered his or her—let's say his—language in the sense that he has developed a metafunctionally organised grammar. This means that he has developed a language system with resources for expressing meanings, which are of three broad kinds: experiential, interpersonal, and textual. In addition, or rather, by definition, the child has learned to use language in a way that is related to the context of situation, the experiential choices he makes reflecting field variables, the interpersonal choices reflecting tenor aspects, and the textual choices reflecting mode considerations.

In terms of what the child can do with language, it means that, unlike the protolinguistic baby, he can give and receive information and can use language to mediate the exchange of goods and services. He can create connected texts, and can engage in discourse that is responsive to what his dialogue partner says in return. He can make reference to past, future, possible, and imaginary worlds, and has a

41

long history behind him of using language as a tool for thought, for expressing his personality, and for organising his view of the world: a language-mediated view of the world, built up and reinforced by countless conversational occasions from birth onwards.

Conscious and unconscious knowledge

Of course, in the process of developing the language, the child has obviously been internalising the **formal** means his language provides for expressing metafunctional meanings. If we switch our focus from what he can do, to what he knows of his language, we could summarise it in the following way:

1. He has internalised the sound system. Evidence for this lies not just in the fact that native speakers understand the sounds he makes, but in his ability to play rhyming games and to invent imaginary names that respect the phonological rules and constraints of syllable structure of the language. Hal and his friends produced names for toys such as *Sheshum*, *Jang*, and *Tabby*, but none like *Pthang* or *Ngabby*.
2. The child has learned morphological rules, evidenced by errors such as *teached* and *sheeps* (see Berko-Gleason, 1958 for research evidence that very young children have a command of the word-formation rules of language).
3. The child has mastered most of the principal syntactic structures of the mother tongue before receiving any formal education, though some formal features take longer than others to be handled with confidence. There are of course some forms that are typical of written language or longer expository monologues, which the child will not yet have had occasion to develop. And 'indirect speech acts' are probably the only common form of 'grammatical metaphor' used, i.e. there are few examples such as *I came to a decision* where an action clause with a locational element supplies the meaning more congruently encoded by the mental process clause *I decided* (see Halliday, 1984, Chapter 10, for a consideration of this area of the grammar of English).
4. The child can also hold orderly conversations where speakers take up their roles by turns. He has indeed had considerable experience in the joint creation of texts.

Most of the aspects of language proficiency I have mentioned are of course part of the child's unconscious knowledge. He will not be able to talk about most of what he 'knows'. For example, while he may differentiate in his speech between *many biscuits* and *much sugar*, he will certainly not be able to talk about 'count' vs. 'noncount' nouns.

Nevertheless, even a pre-school child will have some more conscious understandings and may have developed the first beginnings of a METALANGUAGE with which to talk about language. For example, he may know the terms *rhyme* and *name* as well as being able to play rhyming and naming games. He will certainly have ways of inquiring about things he hasn't grasped, and may use the verb *mean* to do so. Probably, in our literate culture, he knows the term *word*, since this is the unit that becomes more prominent in written language, and if he watches children's TV, has 'educational' toys, or goes out and about in an urban environment, he may well have had occasion to learn what a *letter* is. Certainly, he will have a few names for different genres such as *story*, *fairy story*, *song*, and *nursery rhyme*.

Probably almost all these simple 'technical' terms for talking about aspects of language will have evolved just as naturally as any other area of the lexis, without adult or child feeling that they are marked out in any way. This is worth mentioning because teachers very often feel that a linguistic metalanguage does constitute a special case.

Those who are aware that knowing a language is different from knowing about it, and wish to avoid the possibility of the two being confused, tend to see no place at all in the child's education for developing any explicit awareness of linguistic matters.

Others, taking the opposite view, sometimes behave as though introducing the child to some traditional terms—*noun*, *verb*, *subordinate clause*, and the like—is an automatic means of improving the child's linguistic skills.

I would argue for a more balanced approach, one that is sensitive to the unconscious understandings the child has necessarily developed in the course of learning to speak, and to the fact that there are likely to be at least a few more conscious understandings too. Language may be a phenomenon of just as much interest to the child, as he grows, as other aspects of his world, and need not be a special case in that becoming equipped with ways to talk about it is regarded as inappropriate for this particular phenomenon alone. On the other hand, of course, any metalanguage is developed as a tool to facilitate the exploration and greater understanding of something, and needs to be appropriate to this task and directed towards it.

Learning about language has a place in school.

Limitations of language

It can be seen from the discussion of the child's linguistic abilities and knowledge given in the preceding section that whether we adopt a functional perspective or a more traditional knowledge-oriented one, there are good reasons why children's language development has so often been seen as virtually completed before the child enters school.

What of the negative aspect of the answer, in that case? In what sense do we as adults feel ourselves to be more competent users of language than the primary school child? What does it mean for us to say, as many of us do, that we go on learning our mother tongue for the rest of our lives?

Often our adult superiority is seen in terms of possession of a greater vocabulary and sufficient knowledge to avoid syntactic errors (for example, we don't say *he brang* or *much peanuts*, although six-year-olds frequently do). But if we restrict ourselves to looking at such bits of the lexicogrammar in isolation, then the only things we will be able to offer the child educationally are 'corrections' of such relatively trivial errors, and encouragement to learn new words. Looking at things in this way is what follows from viewing the child's task in developing language as one of learning phonological, syntactic, and/or semantic rules in isolation, and then applying the rules in speech.

My suggestion throughout has been that we see language development as a process of developing resources for expressing meanings, and learning to deploy those resources in an appropriate way. While a school child may have a thorough grasp of all the formal matters discussed earlier, he or she will still be a far more effective communicator at certain times than at others. This is because the child will have had greater experience in some contexts of situation than others. Thus it is in terms of register that the question of language development for the school-age child can be most profitably pursued.

Language development in terms of register

Unfortunately there is as yet no research that can provide illustrative case histories of young children's development of register, although this would be extremely valuable for the consideration of language in educational contexts. In this section, therefore, I propose to clarify the notion of register a little further and make a few general suggestions as to how the child's linguistic abilities can be viewed in such terms.

First let me expand my earlier brief remarks on the three register components: field, tenor, and mode.

Field

This is the component of the situation—the situation viewed as an abstraction—that consists of the activity with which speakers are concerned in the discourse, and/or the subject area of the discourse. The activity is one that has meaning within the culture of the speakers. A sample of fields that adult members of our society might be engaged in may make this clearer. Examples are cooking, gambling, nuclear physics, surfboard riding, fashion, birdwatching, chess, and education. And many of these may have sub-fields (different forms of gambling, of education, etc.) or might be sub-fields of more comprehensive fields (surfboard riding as a form of water sport, itself a kind of sport). I think it is obvious that several of the fields I have listed might not be relevant in another culture. Part of what the child learns (as he or she learns language by hearing and using speech in context) is of course a variety of culture-specific fields; developing language necessarily means developing simultaneously as a member of a cultural group.

As one would expect from this characterisation of field, one of the language systems that expresses it is the experiential one of transitivity (choice of process type: material/mental/relational; presence or absence of the Agent role, etc.). Lexis (other than the strictly attitudinal type) is also a chief means of expressing field, and indeed one gains a good idea of the field of most texts simply by looking at the vocabulary used.

The field of a discourse may in some cases be almost equated with the 'topic', as in a book describing playing strategies in chess. But the field would still be chess if two people were engaged in playing chess at the moment of speaking, and made utterances such as 'your move' or 'don't wobble the table', which would not occur in the other case. The field is the same, but other aspects of the total situational context would be different, and differences in the texts could be explained by those other situational differences.

Field presents the most transparent case for later language development, since we are all consciously aware of the way an initiation into a new field involves extending our linguistic resources. And of course the school plays an obvious role in introducing the child to new fields. This of course is not a matter of teaching new 'content' in isolation. New subject-matter involves language learning too, not just vocabulary development (although this is the most obvious case), but ways of expressing relationships between the phenomena involved, and appropriate genres for conducting investigation and argument within academic fields.

Tenor

This is the component of the situation that concerns relations between speaker and hearer. Cate Poynton is a linguist currently working in this area, and she has proposed that power relations, frequency of contact, and effect are the most important interpersonal dimensions of tenor.

See *Language and Gender* (Poynton, 1989).

Tenor choices tend to be expressed in discourse by features of the interpersonal systems of language, such as the following:

- dialogue or speech role choices (initiator/responder/acknowledger, giver/receiver of goods and services or information)
- mood and tag choices (interrogative/declarative/imperative)
- the expression of attitude (*frankly*; *I think*; *stupid bloody idiot*)
- modality (degrees of possibility: *he might go*; *he will go*)
- modulation (degrees of obligation: *he should go*, etc.)
- vocation (addressing the hearer by name: *Come here, John*; *Darling, you were wonderful*)
- polarity (*yes*; *no*; *no, I didn't*)

Aspects of context relevant to tenor will determine not just the presence, frequency, and form of the expressions of these linguistic features, but how they are distributed between speaker and hearer.

Even the pre-school child who has had little occasion to interact with anyone other than his or her principal care-givers will have had some experience in different kinds of tenor, since the same person will naturally adopt different roles at different times. A parent may on one occasion be adopting the role of pedagogue, and on another, the role of companion in a game of some sort. Thus, the inequality of status inherent in the age difference between parent and child may be very much foregrounded or backgrounded on different occasions, and this will be reflected in the language used. A child who did not vary his or her speech in an appropriate way when confronted with different tenor relations would still have a lot to learn, however many grammatical rules he or she might command.

When it has not been temporarily put aside, the age-related power difference between adult and child allows adults the freedom to direct the course of a conversation with a child, and to interrupt, at will, talk that is going on between children. Children, however, cannot behave in a like manner to adults, and have to develop ways of successfully intruding on conversations between adults, or of being invited to hold the conversational floor (*Do you know what?* is a popular early strategy here).

It may not be until the child enters school that he or she needs to develop ways—including linguistic ways—of expressing peer group solidarity. Probably his or her range of interpersonal epithets and vocatives will expand, enriching the language system, and the system will certainly be deployed in new ways—for purposes of teasing, bullying, face-saving, and the like.

Another new tenor relationship the child will need to become familiar with at school is that between the impersonal author and the generalised reader—rather different from the linguistic interaction of most of their previous experience between a defined 'I' and 'you'. Of course many children will have had plenty of experience with the role of audience for read-aloud stories, but even they will probably not have had much occasion to take on the impersonal authorial role that is more typical of some written genres.

Mode

This is the component of the context that concerns the role language itself plays in the situation. The difference between speech and writing is often cited as a mode difference. If we consider what is involved here, one factor is the distance between speaker and hearer. In a written text, interlocutors are separated in time and space; in a phone conversation, they are separated in space but not time, and face to face there is no physical distance involved.

A related but distinct variable (see Martin, 1983) is the distance between the language produced and the experience it refers to. It may relate to ongoing activity, as would the utterances made in the course of a chess game, or the course of a transaction in a shop. On the other hand, the language may be planning experience in the future, recounting something that has already occurred, or generalising outside specific occasions in time and space. Either spoken or written language could be involved.

These issues are discussed in some detail in *Language, Context, and Text* (Halliday & Hasan, 1989).

All these factors will have some effect on textual choices made by the speakers. The main textual systems of language are those of theme and information, matters of topic/comment and given/new in the clause. In addition, conjunctive items (*and, but, so, in brief, furthermore*), explicitly linking parts of the discourse, and reference items (*that boy; he*) that allude to specific identities in a text, will be related to the mode component. Where both speakers can see the referent in front of them it will not need to be introduced by some locution such as *there was an X*; in other cases it probably will.

Where mode is concerned, the school-age child is relatively inexperienced. As early as the transition phase, the child has used language to recreate or reconsider past events, as well as to talk about future and possible situations. But probably the majority of any young child's linguistic experience will concern the here-and-now situation, and virtually all language addressed to another person will be face to face. (Many four- or five-year-olds become simply speechless when first called on to participate in telephone conversations with familiar addressees.)

It is a familiar experience to many parents to find that they cannot understand what their child tells them about school activities. In this situation, the child's speech is distanced by time from the events he or she is talking of, and the lack of an ongoing shared material context has to be made good by language. It takes some experience in this situation before the child learns to take the needs of the hearer sufficiently into account.

In the following conversation, things are fairly rapidly elucidated.

Example 8.1
[Hal, 5½, has just been fetched from school]
H: You came too soon.
   I was in the middle of a game with the hippopotamus —
M: What hippopotamus?
H: It's got numbers on and you have to try and get them in the numbers, and 60 is the highest—
M: [interrupting] You have to get what in the numbers, darling?
H: What? Um, your ball—on the numbers.
M: I see, you throw it on the hippopotamus.
H: Yes, it's on the wall.

Hal had tried to give too much information at once, and had failed to introduce the various objects and locations involved in a way that enabled his hearer to enter the scene via language—both textual failures related to mode.

The following conversation is one where Hal attempted for a second time to explain a series of events at school that involved his writing a 'spell'—now brought home—that was shown to the head teacher.

Example 8.2
[M, confused, asks H to explain again]
H: You write the spell;
   and you write it in the spider
   and Miss Trevor writes it down
   and you copy off it.
M: Off?
H: From Miss Trevor's writing that she did.
   I did some writing, and she did some writing.
M: Mmm.
H: I did two writings; one in the spider, and one in the um—in the er—
M: ⌠ On the paper.
H: ⌡ ? Book.
   And I did the first writing . . . [he tails off]
M: And then you took it to Mrs Burrows.
H: Yeah.
   No. That was another [? day. Today]
M: That was what?
   Another day?
H: Mm; today.

Note: ⌠ indicates simultaneous speech

47

Although I never understood what the spider was, and only realised at the end that the events had taken place over a longer period than the day he brought the spell home, we can see him using his linguistic resources as judiciously as possible. Instead of the original gabble of information (not given here), he tries to chunk it up appropriately, and to be explicit (*I did two writings*, etc.), recognising something of why his original account had failed.

This initial language failure was not a matter of getting any structural rules wrong, but resulted from a lack of experience in this context of situation. How he learned to take greater account of the hearer's needs, when distanced from the experience described, was by gradually creating a more satisfactory text with the help of his addressee.

Examples 8.1 and 8.2 show problems arising when using language to describe an experience that is at a distance. The other dimension of mode—distance from the addressee when producing language—is an important aspect of the child's task when learning to write, and here of course he or she cannot repair any communicative failures in the process of a dialogue.

Beyond the context of situation

The model of language I have been building up in the course of this book is one of the linguistic system organised into three broad sets of meaning choices. These sets of options and their expressions in terms of words and structures constitute the metafunctional components of the language. For any piece of discourse, choices within each component will be affected by features of the context of situation. Aspects of field will affect experiential linguistic choices; tenor choices will affect interpersonal linguistic choices; and mode variables will affect textual linguistic choices.

Components of the situational context influence the speaker's selection of linguistic options.

Part of what is involved in becoming a speaker of a language involves selecting linguistic options that are sensitive to these contextual variables. This is what is meant by learning to use language appropriately.

Further than this, we need to recognise that field, tenor, and mode choices themselves may be influenced by something else, and this is the genre in which the text occurs (see Martin, 1984). The term GENRE can here be taken to include not only traditional literary genres such as narrative, sonnet, or novel, and non-literary written forms such as reports and letters of various kinds, but also spoken discourses. Any goal-oriented activity accomplished with the mediation of language can be regarded as a genre. Examples of spoken genres would range from making a purchase to making a speech.

A very detailed discussion of the structure of genres—particularly those of casual conversation, is provided by Hasan in Language, Context, and Text *(Halliday & Hasan, 1989).*

Every genre will have its own particular shape—its variation on beginning-middle-end structure. The choice of genre may affect the language used directly (for example, *Once upon a time* is indexical of the fairy story genre); or genre choice can affect the language used indirectly. This will be by influencing field, tenor, and mode choices made as the discourse proceeds. For example, if the genre—the purposeful activity—is the sale of an item such as a motor car, the speaker trying to effect the sale may adopt a series of roles over the course of the negotiation. Initially, a deferential, 'powerless' role may be taken up; this may give way to the role of vehicle expert (assigning the addressee the role of novice), and perhaps finally the speaker may adopt an authoritative role offering hire purchase loans to a suppliant buyer. These changes in tenor will be reflected in the interpersonal linguistic options expressed by both interlocutors.

Clearly when we take into account the mature and proficient language user's ability to deploy language effectively in a variety of contexts of situation and a variety of spoken and written genres, it makes no sense to regard the five-year-old as having completed his language learning, or indeed to see the achievement of literacy simply in terms of a skill involving the substitution of letters for sounds.

Postscript

In this book I have attempted to suggest a way of looking at language as a set of resources for making meanings. By looking at a case history of one child's development of such a system, I hope to have shown what is distinctive about human language and how instances of language in use (texts) are related in a very specific way to the contexts that give rise to them. This helps to explain both how the child comes to learn his or her mother tongue, and how the adult, in using it, manages to do all that he or she does with language.

I have made no attempt here to suggest how you should go about providing your students in the classroom with opportunities to extend their linguistic resources and learn to deploy them most appropriately. Nor have I offered any critique of language development materials— such as literacy programs—actually used in schools, or of the kinds of discourses actually produced in formal teaching situations.

You own professional experience and expertise will have much to contribute here, and I hope that an appreciation of the nature of language and the child's task in developing it, will prove a fruitful basis for more direct consideration of the use of language in specifically educational contexts.

References

Austin, J., *How to do Things with Words* (Oxford University Press, New York, 1962).

Bates, E., *The Emergence of Symbols* (Academic Press, New York, 1979).

Berko-Gleason, J., 'The child's learning of English morphology', *Word* **14**, reprinted in L. Bloom (ed.), *Readings in Language Development* (Wiley, New York, 1978).

Braine, M., 'The ontogeny of English phrase structure: The first phase', *Language* **39**, 1963, pp. 1-13.

Brown, R., & Bellugi, U., 'Three processes in the child's acquisition of syntax', *Harvard Educational Review* **34**, 1964, pp. 133-51.

Bruner, J.S., 'The ontogenesis of speech acts', *Journal of Child Language* **2**, 1975, pp. 1-19.

Carter, A.L., 'Prespeech meaning relations', in P. Fletcher & M. Garman (eds.), *Language Acquisition* (Cambridge University Press, Cambridge, 1979), pp. 71-92.

Chomsky, N., *Syntactic Structures* (Mouton, The Hague, 1957).

Chomsky, N., *Aspects of the Theory of Syntax* (Massachusetts Institute of Technology Press, Cambridge, 1965).

Cross, T., 'Mothers' speech adjustments: The contribution of selected child listener variables', in C.E. Snow & C.A. Ferguson (eds.), *Talking to Children: Language Input and Acquisition* (Cambridge University Press, Cambridge, 1977), pp. 151-5.

Dore, J., 'Holophrases, speech acts and language universals', *Journal of Child Language* **2**, 1975, pp. 21-40.

Greenfield, P.M., Nelson, K., & Saltzman, E., 'The development of rulebound strategies for manipulating seriated cups: A parallel between action and grammar', *Cognitive Psychology* **3**, 1972, pp. 291-310.

Greenfield, P.M., & Smith, J.H., *The Structure of Communication in Early Language Development* (Academic Press, New York, 1976).

Halliday, M.A.K., *Learning How to Mean: Explorations in the Development of Language* (Edward Arnold, London, 1975).

Halliday, M.A.K., *System and Function in Language: Selected Papers*, ed. G. Kress (Oxford University Press, London, 1976).

Halliday, M.A.K., *Language as Social Semiotic: The Social Interpretation of Language and Meaning* (Edward Arnold, London, 1978).

Halliday, M.A.K., 'The development of texture in children', in T. Myers (ed.), *The Development of Conversation and Discourse* (Edinburgh University Press, Edinburgh, 1979).

Halliday, M.A.K., *A Short Introduction to Functional Grammar* (Edward Arnold, London, 1984).

Halliday, M.A.K., & Hasan, R., *Language, Context, and Text: Aspects of Language in a Social-semiotic Perspective* (Oxford University Press, Oxford, 1989).

Ingram, D., 'Transitivity in child language', *Language* **47**, 1971, pp. 888-910.

Lemke, J.L., *Using Language in the Classroom* (Oxford University Press, Oxford, 1989).

Lock, A. (ed.), *Action, Gesture and Symbol: the Emergence of Language* (Academic Press, London, 1978).

Martin, J.R., 'The development of register', in J. Fine & R.O. Freedle (eds.), *Developmental Issues in Discourse* (Ablex, Norwood, New Jersey, 1983, pp. 1-39.

Martin, J.R., 'Language, register and genre', in *Children Writing: Reader*, ECT418 Language Studies (Deakin University, Victoria, 1984), pp.21-30.

Newport, E., 'Motherese: The speech of mothers to young children', *Child Development* **44**, 1976, pp. 497-504.

Painter, C., *Into the Mother Tongue: A Case Study in Early Language Development* (Pinter, London, 1984).

Poynton, C., *Language and Gender: Making the Difference* (Oxford University Press, Oxford, 1989).

Poynton, C., 'Names as vocatives: Forms and functions', *Nottingham Linguistic Circular* **13**, 1984, pp. 1−34.

Schlesinger, I.M., 'Learning grammar: From pivot to realisation rule', in R. Huxley & E. Ingram (eds.), *Language Acquisition* (Academic Press, London, 1971), pp. 79-89.

Snow, C.E., & Ferguson, C.A. (eds.), *Talking to Children: Language Input and Acquisition* (Cambridge University Press, Cambridge, 1977).

Waterson, N., & Snow, C. (eds.), *The Development of Communication* (Wiley, New York, 1978).

Further reading

Bullowa, M. (ed.), *Before Speech: The Beginning of Interpersonal Communication* (Cambridge University Press, Cambridge, 1979).
An interesting collection of readings that examines recent research into the earliest bases of interpersonal communication. From birth, infants begin to learn the complex patterns of interaction particular to their culture, and in the process they prepare for the learning of speech.

Halliday, M.A.K., *Learning How to Mean: Explorations in the Development of Language* (Edward Arnold, London, 1975).
This is the volume in which Halliday first suggested that learning one's mother tongue is a process of learning 'how to mean'. In offering a discussion of the very early language development of one child, Nigel, Halliday sought to demonstrate the relationship of the emergent language of the child to the full language system he would ultimately learn to use.

Lock, A. (ed.), *Action, Gesture and Symbol* (Academic Press, London, 1978).
An interesting collection on neonatal and infant developmental studies. Papers by Newson, Trevarthen, and Shotter are especially valuable as a background to the protolanguage phase.

Myers, T. (ed.), *The Development of Conversation and Discourse* (Edinburgh University Press, Edinburgh, 1979).
The learning of conversation is for the infant a necessary part of the process of learning to interact with others. This collection of papers looks at some of the research in this area.

Rogers, S. (ed.), *Children and Language: Readings in Early Language and Socialization* (Oxford University Press, London, 1975).
A set of readings on early language learning. The papers collected here are drawn from a variety of different disciplines, all exploring both the social purposes served in learning language and the associated implications for our views of personal identity.

Snow, C.A., & Ferguson, C. (eds.), *Talking to Children: Language Input and Acquisition* (Cambridge University Press, Cambridge, 1977).
A collection of papers on investigations of baby-talk. It contains some interesting material, but is disappointing in that so little of the research is informed by discourse-analysis techniques, which could provide the most powerful insights into the role of the adult interlocuter in language development.

Tough, J., *Focus on Meaning* (Allen & Unwin, London, 1973).
Tough is not a linguist, so that the research methods she used to examine children's language development were different from those described in this book. However, there are useful parallels between her work and some of what is discussed here. In particular, Tough is interested in examining patterns of interaction and of talk experienced by children in pre-school situations, and in exploring the kinds of classroom strategies teachers may pursue in order to assist young children learn the language of school learning.

Bernstein, B., *Class, Codes and Control*, vol. 2, *Applied Studies Towards a Sociology of Language* (Routledge & Kegan Paul, London, 1973).
All the papers in this collection provide useful discussions of the influence of parenting and early patterns of interaction upon children and their language and learning. The papers in Part I are particularly relevant.

Wells, G., 'Language as interaction', in G. Wells (ed.), *Learning through Interaction: The Study of Language Development* (Cambridge University Press, Cambridge, 1981), pp. 22-72.

Wells, G., 'Apprenticeship in meaning', in K. Nelson (ed.), *Children's Language* (Gardner Press, New York, 1980), pp. 45-126.
Wells is more eclectic in his approach to his research and in the kinds of orientations he adopts than is the author of this book. Hence, though there are parallels between a number of his observations and those here, there are also important differences.

Technical terms